NIGHT OF THE LIVING YOGURT

D1516952

Other Avon Camelot Books by
William L. DeAndrea and Matthew DeAndrea

WHEN DINOSAURS RULED THE BASEMENT

Avon Books are available at special quantity discounts for bulk purchases for sales promotions, premiums, fund raising or educational use. Special books, or book excerpts, can also be created to fit specific needs.

For details write or telephone the office of the Director of Special Markets, Avon Books, Dept. FP, 1350 Avenue of the Americas, New York, New York 10019, 1-800-238-0658.

NIGHT OF THE LIVING YOGURT

WILLIAM L. DeANDREA
and MATTHEW DeANDREA

AN AVON  CAMELOT BOOK

If you purchased this book without a cover, you should be aware that this book is stolen property. It was reported as "unsold and destroyed" to the publisher, and neither the author nor the publisher has received any payment for this "stripped book."

NIGHT OF THE LIVING YOGURT is an original publication of Avon Books. This work has never before appeared in book form.

AVON BOOKS
A division of
The Hearst Corporation
1350 Avenue of the Americas
New York, New York 10019

Copyright © 1996 by William L. DeAndrea and Matthew DeAndrea
Published by arrangement with the authors
Library of Congress Catalog Card Number: 95-96057
ISBN: 0-380-78358-4
RL: 4.1

All rights reserved, which includes the right to reproduce this book or portions thereof in any form whatsoever except as provided by the U.S. Copyright Law. For information address Jane Rotrosen Agency, 318 East 51st Street, New York, New York 10022.

First Avon Camelot Printing: June 1996

CAMELOT TRADEMARK REG. U.S. PAT. OFF. AND IN OTHER COUNTRIES, MARCA REGISTRADA, HECHO EN U.S.A.

Printed in the U.S.A.

OPM   10   9   8   7   6   5   4   3   2   1

To Grandpa—
we miss you

PROLOGUE

The monster reached out a gooey white "hand" and grabbed for me.

It was at least seven feet tall, whitish and bulky, with a shape that was always changing, but was always based on the shape of a human. It was as if someone had taken Frankenstein's monster and dipped him in runny white frosting or something.

Gemma, Michael, and I had sneaked into the school to find out what was causing all the weird things that had been plaguing the place, and now we had learned. We'd discovered the creature's secret, and now it was hunting us through the darkened corridors.

It had chased us down the hallway from the home ec kitchen, each step making a gooshy, sliding, sucking sound. You wouldn't have thought it could move very fast, big as it was, but we couldn't seem to gain any ground on it. We were afraid to look back as we ran.

"The library!" my little brother Michael said. "We can lock him out." Nobody is supposed to know this, but Mr. Nathans, the school librarian, gave Michael a key to get in. He's a seven-year-old genius, you see, and Mr. Nathans said it would be a crime to keep him away from books. I don't think he or Michael ever thought he'd be using the key to try to save our lives.

The library is a big room, three times the size of an ordinary classroom, and it has doors at either end. Naturally, we went to the closer one.

We waited outside the door while Michael started fumbling through his pockets. He came up with a yo-yo, three rubber bands, four X-Men Pogs, and a wad of Kleenex, but no keys.

The creature slurped toward us. In a way, it was fascinating to watch it. It didn't walk so much as skate, and where the "legs" touched, they merged, only separating enough to allow the thing to move forward. In the same way, it only seemed to have arms when it wanted to reach for something.

And it had no face at all. That was the spookiest part. How could it see us? How did it know where it was going?

We never did learn the answer to that, but it sure did know where it was going—it was going straight for us.

Gemma was watching it with me, while Michael kept searching for the key. "Um, you'd better hurry, there, squirt," she said. "Or we better run again, and forget the library."

"Here it is!" Michael said.

Gemma and I expressed the same sentiment: "Whew!"

"*Oh*," Michael said. "This is the key to the school's east door that I stole."

I wanted to scream. I wanted to cry. I wanted to grab Michael by the ankles and shake the darned key out of him.

The monster was about twenty feet away then Michael finally found the key; he was about ten feet away when he got the door open. He was so close behind us when we ducked inside the door and closed it, that there was a double thump—first the door slammed into the doorjamb, then the creature splatted up against the door.

And *splat* was the right word. The pebble-glass window to the hallway was suddenly covered with a flat sheet of whiteness.

Gemma and I leaned up against the door for a few seconds while Michael locked it. As big as the creature was, we expected to have to use all our strength against the bulk of it, but it didn't really seem to be pushing.

We all took deep breaths, and made some crooked grins at each other, as if congratulating ourselves on our escape.

"Okay," I said. "Now we know what we're up against. We're locked in here. We can stay here until morning, if we have to."

Gemma was looking at the door. When she turned to me, there was a sick look in her green eyes. "I don't think we can, Jon."

"Sure we can," I said. "Look, it's going away. It doesn't even fill up the whole window anymore."

Gemma didn't say anything; she just pointed to the floor in front of the doorway.

A pool of foul-smelling whiteness was oozing under the door. It didn't spread out evenly. It began bunching up, and forming a shape. A sort of Frankenstein's monster shape.

Michael still had the key in his hand. "Out the other door," I said. "Hurry. I'll try to slow him down."

Michael, interested in everything, asked me how I was going to do that. I told him I'd tell him later. That might give me some time to think of it myself.

3

I looked around the room. Maybe there was a fire extinguisher that I could use to freeze it's feet or something. Maybe I could try—

Too late. The creature was fully formed and ready for me. Deep within itself, it made a kind of bubbling sound that was like a wet roar.

"Go," I said, pushing Michael and Gemma toward the door. "Go. Leave the school. Get help."

They went. The creature came forward, slowly, now, as if it was playing with me. I ran behind Mr. Nathans's desk, trying to keep it between me and the creature, hoping to get away if it tried to chase me around the desk.

Even as I did it, I knew how dumb I was. A creature who can ooze through a crack under a doorway could certainly ooze over the top of a desk.

Which was exactly what it started to do. In desperation, I reached out to the desk to grab something— anything to save myself. This was equally stupid. Even if there'd been a machete there, or a machine gun, or some other kind of deadly weapon, I doubt it would have had much effect on this thing.

It was stupid, but I got lucky. Mr. Nathans has asthma and allergies and all kinds of things, and he's always got stuff for it all over his desk. My desperate grab had snagged a can of aerosol spray he kept around to kill germs on the phone so he wouldn't get a sore throat. I think the can said ANTISEPTIC. What did I have to lose? In another second, I'd be trapped in the hug of suffocating goo. It was already growing "arms." I pulled off the cap and sprayed where its eyes ought to have been.

When the green liquid hit it, it made that bubble-roar again, and drew back.

4

It only gave me a split second, but I was ready to use it. I dashed out from around the desk.

Now I had a problem. I could get to the door we'd come in by, but that was locked. And the creature was between me and the door Michael and Gemma had left by, the one that was open. By now I knew it didn't like whatever was in this can, but I didn't know if I had enough of it to destroy the thing, or even to keep it at bay long enough for me to get out of the room.

Meanwhile, I kept backing up toward the far wall, the one with the high bookshelves and the rolling ladders against it, squirting the monster from time to time to keep him back. I sneaked a quick look over my shoulder, and came up with a plan. I backed toward the corner of the room, then, when I was close to the wall, I sprinted with all my might toward one of the rolling ladders about fifteen feet away. Running as fast as I could, I leaped onto the ladder and scooted down the wall too fast for the creature to cut me off, but not too fast for it to snake out an impossibly long fake "arm" and slap my can away. I was sorry it was gone, but I wasn't about to go back to look for it.

I ran to the door Gemma and Michael had left by, dashed through it, and what do you think I found? *Gemma and Michael!*

"Is this the way you two follow orders?"

"Who appointed you to give orders?" Gemma said.

"We were worried about you," Michael added.

"Well, let's get out of here. That's a suggestion, okay?"

Gemma smiled. "And a very sensible one, too."

"Thank you," I said. "It takes the thing a little while to ooze under the door. We ought to be able to make it to the west exit by then."

5

"Let's go."

We might really have been able to make the west exit in the time it took the monster to ooze under the door, but I'll never know, because it didn't ooze under the door.

Instead, like an avalanche of slush, it threw its wet self against the door and popped the lock. It gushed out into the corridor, and in a few seconds, it was its old Frankenstein self again. The chase resumed, and this time, I wasn't sure we would ever get out of this alive.

It all started last week, when the class bell rang, and the clock began to run backward.

It was the ringing of the bell that got us all looking at the clock. We had just sat down in Mrs. Simpkins's math class so nobody would expect to hear a bell so soon.

You never expected time to fly in math class, but it was flying now, in reverse. The hands of the built-in wall clock over the door zoomed backward through the hours so rapidly you could hear them spinning once the bell stopped. The rest of the class, Abdul, Biff, Stacy, Linda, Bob, and everybody else started to laugh. All but Gemma Davis and me, Jonathan Parlo. The two of us had seen weird stuff before in this town, stuff that could have killed us, the people of Marsdentown, and maybe even the whole earth. Nobody believed us, but we'd seen it and fought it, and even defeated it, for a while at least.

Maybe, a shaky voice inside me said, *that while is up.*

I looked around the room, expecting anything to happen. If there'd been a fleet of flying saucers outside the window landing on the baseball field, I wouldn't have been surprised. If Mrs. Simpkins's hair started turning from gray to black, and all the kids were shrinking into toddlers, I would have nodded, then gone looking for a mirror to see how young *I* was getting.

But I didn't see anything like that. All I saw was a bunch of kids laughing and pointing at the clock.

Even though Mrs. Simpkins is not the kind of teacher who has a gift of making Venn diagrams or fractions exciting, she's basically a nice lady, so when she started banging on her desk with a ruler, I knew we had really gotten out of hand.

"*Class!*" she said sharply. "That's enough! Obviously, there's some malfunction in the central clockworks in the main office." She looked around the room. "Gemma . . . and Jon. You seem to be able to control yourselves. Please go to the office and inform them of what's happened. I think I can trust the two of you to do it without giggling."

Well, you know how it is when a bunch of kids gets the giggles. Anything Mrs. Simpkins said about it would just make it worse. She hit the desk with her ruler again, and the giggles subsided, at least a little.

Gemma and I walked to her desk and stood there while she scribbled out a pass for us. I took one last look at the clock whizzing its way into the past as I went out into the hall.

"She must have read my mind," Gemma said. She rubbed her short red hair the way she does when she's worried, and I could see fear in her green eyes. "When that stuff started happening, I thought, 'I've got to talk this over with Jon.' "

"Yeah," I said. "I wanted to talk to you, too, but we don't have too long to do it. She wrote the time on

8

the pass. If we take too long to get to the office, we'll catch it from Mr. Calstone, for sure."

"Mr. Calstone?" Gemma said impatiently. "Forget Mr. Calstone. What difference does one grumpy vice-principal make when the earth is being invaded?"

I looked at her. "Do you think so?" I asked. "You think the Twisters are trying again?"

Gemma looked miserable. "I don't know. Things have been so normal since we first fought them, sometimes I can make the whole thing seem like a dream. No, not a dream, like a story around the fire at camp. But then something strange happens, and I'm sure they're coming back. What do you think?"

"I don't know," I said miserably. "One thing I thought of when I saw the clock going backward was that instead of coming here, they were drawing us back to *them* this time."

"I'm sorry I asked," Gemma said.

"It doesn't seem to be happening, though. Things are going along the usual way. It still seems to be June. The flowers are still on the shrub outside the window. Nothing weird is happening to the sky. I just don't know what's going on."

"That's the trouble. With the Twisters, they could be up to anything."

That was the trouble, all right.

I think I'd better fill you in on the background here.

Gemma and Michael and I live in Marsdentown. It's one of the nicest places to live in you could ever imagine. We have snow in the winter, and it's hot enough to swim in Bullseye Lake in the summertime. There are parks and playgrounds, and the Marsdentown School, which we all attend (Gemma and I in the seventh grade, Michael in the second) is constantly named one of the best in the state. Even though it's a small town, all kinds of people live here, and we all mostly get along. There's very little crime.

But, as the three of us learned a few months ago, although it's one of the nicest places on earth, Marsdentown is also one of the most dangerous places in the universe. Michael tried to explain it to me once.

Michael, I should tell you, is a typical seven-year-old kid, except that he happens to be a genius. For example, he'll watch *Power Rangers* and then work out equations on how Lord Zed might actually send those creatures of his to earth for the Power Rangers to fight. And the equations are real. One time Professor Heimrich of Princeton University showed up on our doorstep because he couldn't believe a seven year old had actually written him the letter Michael had sent to him about something called "wormhole ablation." Michael tried to explain it to me, but I'm not a genius, and I couldn't pass it on to you even if you are.

Anyway, he also tried to explain to me what makes our home town such a dangerous place.

"See, Jon, Marsdentown happens to lie on a point in hyperdimensional space where the vibratory resonances of a whole bunch of different universes come closest together."

I told him I didn't get it.

He got that serious look he gets when he's trying to explain something. I think deep down, Michael thinks we're all as smart as he is, but for some reason we've decided to play dumb just to frustrate him.

This time, he decided to play along. "Okay. You know how there's that place to the west of town where Marsdentown, Windsor, Booneville, and Sewanaka all meet? Well, Marsdentown is like that, only with universes. We can't ordinarily detect the others, because their dimensional vibrations are different.''

I think I sort of, kind of, maybe understood that because I read a lot of science fiction. Gemma's father is a science fiction writer, and he gives me a lot of stuff for free. What I boiled it down to was that if you're moving between universes, Marsdentown is the easiest place in ours to land.

That's where the Twisters come in. Michael gave them that name because of the way they walk. The Twisters are creatures that look like mutated palm trees, about eight feet tall, with four broad, flat tentacles on the bottom to walk on, and four long, round tentacles at the top to grab things with. They had green, lime-looking things between each of their upper tentacles that we guess are eyes, and a mouth on the top of their ''heads,'' between the tentacles.

The Twisters come from an ancient civilization that has so polluted its home planet that only a ruthless dictatorship keeps them alive. A group of Twisters stole some space-and-time warp equipment and came to earth.

But their universe is older than ours, and the earth they came to was the earth of our distant past, the late Jurassic period. They established a base there, but they have no interest in ruling a wilderness. It's been so long since their planet had any wilderness, they wouldn't know what to do with it, anyway. What the Twisters want to conquer is the earth of today, now. By their standards, it's practically empty, and the metal they need has already been mined, and buildings they can use are already up. To take over, all they have to do is wipe us out.

They've got machines that can do it, but it takes some time to set those up. They need two days alone in the

Marsdentown of the present to build their machines. To do that, they have to get all, or at least most, of the people out of Marsdentown.

Their first plan was to send some dinosaurs from the Jurassic period through the time warp, and have them eat and stomp and scare us to death, literally. Fortunately, a freak vibration in the Parlo household opened a small warp in our basement before they were ready. Gemma, Michael, and I went through the warp and learned about the Twisters. They captured us, and tried to get us to betray the earth, but we managed to escape, wreck a lot of their equipment, get back to our own time, and close down the warp before they could get through after us.

You probably don't believe any of that. Nobody does. We were so busy trying to save our own necks, we forgot to get any proof. Even Gemma's father doesn't believe us, and you'd think *he'd* have an open mind, since he spends all day imagining alien societies. All he did when we told him was to split his beard with a big grin and tell me to write it down. Which I did. He helped me get it published in a book called *When Dinosaurs Ruled the Basement,* but the publisher insisted on calling it "fiction," which is pretty insulting if you ask me.

So there we were, Gemma and I, walking down the hallway, thinking the Twisters were going to try again, scared to death, and feeling very alone.

"I wish the squirt were here," Gemma said. "Then we could talk about this all together."

I agreed. One thing Michael never ran out of was ideas.

The Marsdentown School is built like a short letter T with a long, long crossbar. Grades K-4 are located on the left part of the crossbar, and 5-8 on the right part with the library right where they meet. The short stem of the ''T'' houses the gym, cafeteria and kitchen, and the administrative offices.

No sooner did Gemma and I hit the wide hallway where the stem and crossbar joined, then up popped Michael like a genie from a lamp. Actually, he popped out of the second grade room doorway, but the timing was still pretty amazing.

All the way down the hall we'd heard the sounds of kids giggling and teachers yelling (well, a few of the cooler teachers seemed to be laughing, too) but we hadn't seen anybody else in the hallway.

''We were just talking about you, baby brother,'' I said. ''What are you doing out of class?''

''What about you?'' he asked.

Gemma grinned at him. She likes Michael, but teases him a lot. ''We're off to see the wizard about the clock in our room. Now answer the question, squirt.''

''It's going crazy in our room, too, and I couldn't help thinking about—you know.''

''We know, all right.''

''Boy,'' Michael said fervently. ''I hope we're all wrong. Anyway, I decided I needed to get a look at that clock.''

''How'd you manage that?'' Gemma wanted to know.

Michael shrugged. ''I told Miss Zoconty that I had an idea what was wrong with the clock, and I might be able to tell them how to fix it.''

Gemma scowled. ''What is wrong with it?''

''How should I know? When she asked me, I gave her some doubletalk.'' Michael frowned. ''When people believe you're a genius, you can tell them anything. It's not nice, but very tempting.''

You also, I could see, have worries other people don't have.

It's hard to keep Michael down. He shook off his worries, and said, "Anyway, the class was so unruly, she was willing to take any step to get the clock fixed, so she wrote me a pass and sent me on my way."

"Do you think Mr. Calstone is going to let you look at the clock?"

"You may have to distract him while I sneak into the inner office."

"Oh, right," Gemma said. "He's grouchy enough as it is. All we need is for him to catch us pulling a trick on him."

"I thought he didn't count when the earth is being invaded."

"Oh, yeah," Gemma said. "I forgot. Okay, squirt, you can count on us."

If Michael weren't around, Gemma would be the smartest kid I ever knew. She is absolutely the best at dealing with grownups. But even she got nervous whenever she had to deal with Mr. Calstone.

Homer Calstone used to be a teacher at Marsdentown School—history, my best subject. I'm glad he became assistant principal before I came along, because he is *strict*. I guess every school has to have a disciplinarian, but they don't have to enjoy the job so much. It's not that he's cruel or unfair. It's just the way he gives you this narrow-eyed grin and uses his voice like a church organist when he says things like, "Throwing a football in the *hall,* Mr. Parlo? And breaking a light fixture? Three days *detention.*" It's that little extra emphasis he puts on the word "detention" that really gets you.

People old enough to remember say that Mr. Calstone was easier to get a long with, even as assistant principal, back before the old principal, Mr. Zimmerman, retired. Mr. Calstone, apparently, was drooling for the job and was very upset when they brought in Mrs. Vanling from Booneville to be the new principal.

Be that as it may, it made him pretty sour on life, and since his job was making kids behave, misbehavior at Marsdentown School was a pretty sour experience. I suppose that actually worked to keep us young animals in line, because it was no fun to experience.

But there was something else. Mr. Calstone didn't like Michael.

Well, that might be going a bit too far—Mr. Calstone, after all, didn't seem to like much of anybody. But he sure wasn't *comfortable* around Michael. It was as if having a kid around who was smarter than he was, was one more irritation than he was willing to stand.

Every parents' night at school, Mr. Calstone would be buzzing around Mom, saying that it wasn't really good for Michael to have to be held to the pace of the other children, and that Michael's being so smart was bad for the other children's self-esteem.

If our dad was alive, I don't know what he'd do if he heard Mr. Calstone saying stuff like that—probably something loud and angry. Mom, though, is a lawyer, and she can out-argue anybody, especially when she's right.

After Professor Heimrich came by, Mr. Calstone started getting especially pushy about it, saying maybe Princeton would accept Michael, and set up a program for him, and stuff like that.

Dad probably would have stuffed him in a garbage can at that point, but Mom just said, "My son needs as normal a life as possible. His teacher says he's accepted by the other children, and works and plays well with them. Any extra mental work he needs, I provide him. You might feel better knowing that Professor Heimrich has worked out a study program for Michael, and he follows it on his own time. In the meantime, he plays tag in the playground and talks about cartoons at lunchtime. He doesn't feel like a freak, Mr. Calstone. He feels lucky. I think you'll agree that that's a good way for a child to feel. Or don't you?''

Of course, once Mom put it that way, he had to say he did agree, but the tight twist his lips got every time he saw my brother just got tighter and more twisted after that. We were about to see that look any second, now, because we'd arrived at the main office.

Except that we didn't. Mr. Calstone was there, all right, standing right in the doorway, but he was different, somehow. He was . . . relaxed. Instead of standing rigid with his arms folded across his chest in the usual way, he was leaning against the doorframe with his feet crossed at the ankles. Instead of the tight line his lips usually made, now they were spread in a friendly smile. One of the dark hairs he kept plastering and replastering across his bald spot was loose, and he just left it there.

And instead of glaring at us for a couple of seconds, to make sure we knew we were mere children and he was a Big Shot, he waved a casual hand and said, ''Hi, kids, what can I do for you?''

We were all pretty shocked. Gemma, as usual, got over it first, but when she spoke, she sounded like Dorothy meeting the Wizard of Oz for the first time.

''Hello, Mr. Calstone. We, um, that is, Jon and I, um, Mrs. Simpkins sent us to find out if you know that the clock in our room is gong crazy.''

''I know about it. Is that weird or what?'' He shook his head at the wonder of it.

I was ready to shake my head in wonder, too. I was wondering if time had run backward for Mr. Calstone, and brought him back to a time before he got to be such a grump.

"And what about you, little fella?" he said to Michael. "Keeping your big brother company?" Even his voice sounded different.

"Not exactly," Michael said. "Miss Zoconty sent me because I told her I think I know how to fix the clock."

"Well," said this imposter, "if anybody could do it, I bet you're the one. The thing is, it's not broken anymore."

"Oh," I said.

"Stopped whizzing backward about a minute ago. You must have been on the way. I was just about to set it back to the right time. Want to have a look at it first, Michael?"

Michael had been staring at the assistant principal's face with that little storm-cloud look he gets when he's concentrating.

"Michael?" Mr. Calstone repeated. "Would you like to have a look?"

"Huh? Oh, sure. I mean, yes, sir. I would."

He ushered all three of us into his office, pausing only to give Mrs. Vanling a cheerful hello through the open door of her office. She didn't look too cheerful, herself; she looked distracted, but Mr. Calstone ignored that. He unlocked a panel built into the wall and revealed the master clock and its workings. Michael looked closely.

"There's a little bit of a scorch here at the main lead, see it?"

I saw it. I may not be a genius, but I'm pretty good with gadgets. "Michael," I said, "do you think the

17

polarity of the electricity got reversed somehow? That can make this kind of clock run backward.''

''That's what it looks like,'' Michael said. ''Only you saw how fast those hands were turning. How could such a surge of power only have affected the clock?''

''And the bells,'' Gemma said. ''Don't forget the bells.''

''Well,'' Mr. Calstone said, ''whatever the answer to our little mystery is, it will have to wait till later. Time to go back to class, now kids.''

That was the second time I'd heard him say the word ''kids'' in the last five minutes. I wouldn't make a big deal out of that, except for the fact that it was also the second time I'd ever heard him use the word in my life.

We went back out through the office. He said another cheery hello to the principal, interrupting Mrs. Vanling's conversation with Mrs. Jackson (our friend Abdul's mother) who was the school secretary. They were looking at Mr. Calstone strangely. He didn't seem to notice.

He shepherded us out to the hall, said, ''Bye, kids,'' (that made three) and sent us on our way. We were about five steps away from the office when Gemma remembered something.

''Mr. Calstone,'' she said. ''You forgot to check our hall passes.''

''Don't worry about it,'' he said. ''Have a nice day!''

With things getting as weird as this, I kind of doubted I would.

2

In fact, it didn't turn out to be so bad. With the end of school approaching, we were too busy to be worried. In the first place, we had to get back to math class and make sure we had the assignment. Then, after school, I had a ball game, and Gemma had a piano lesson. She plays four different instruments, and her knowledge of music really helped us against the Twisters. Mom would pick Michael up, and he'd be home doing this week's batch of equations to be mailed to New Jersey for Professor Heimrich to go over.

Then there was the Marsdentown School Spring Festival. Mrs. Vanling started that five years ago, when she came in as principal. Every year she selects a theme, and the whole school has to do something in honor of it.

Sometimes, that can be fun. Like last year, she selected ''Flight,'' and we got an astronaut to come to the school to speak at the big dinner that wraps everything up. My class researched things and made all kinds of paper airplanes and put on a show of stunt flying and accuracy, duration of flight, and things like that.

This year was important, but not so much fun, at least for me. The theme was "Ecology," and this year, along with the projects and the reports and the exhibitions and the rest, Mrs. Vanling had a new brainstorm—this year's dinner would be prepared and served by the kids themselves.

And not just any old dinner. This was to be a completely organic, low fat, low cholesterol, ecologically friendly meal. One bite of it, and you would live forever.

Not really, but you'd deserve to, considering the work that went into it. All the home ec classes were taking part, including mine. At Marsdentown school, all the kids, boys and girls, take home ec *and* shop, which Gemma and I agree is a neat idea. I like to cook, and she says hammering nails is a great way to take out your aggressions.

So, okay, I like to cook. But out of a menu of soy-burgers, organically grown green beans, and carrots, filtered water and for dessert, school-made non-fat yogurt, what do you think *I* got? The green beans.

Some cooking. Boil water. Steam beans. Serve. The cooking was nothing—the growing was the pits. First, we had to reclaim a plot of land out past the edge of the ball field. Then we got the soil ready, planted, watered, and so on and so on. Since this was organic, we could only use "natural fertilizer," and I will spare you the unpleasant details of *that*.

If you're growing something organic, you can't use pesticides, either. You either have a lot of beans with worm bites in them, or you get out there every day and pick the little green stinkers off the plants with your fingers.

We got a little help in that part of it. Michael recruited a bunch of second grade friends to pick worms with us, and they were good—sharp eyes, and quick little fingers. Unfortunately, Mrs. Vanling made them stop. They were squooshing too many of them in the playground, and using the rest to scare other kids.

Anyway, I couldn't wait for next week when we'd harvest the things and eat them—the beans, I mean, not the worms, although I'm not too sure I'd put that past Michael's gang, either. Michael once announced in the middle of dinner, "If you ate a big bug like a cockroach or something, it would probably taste like lobster." He would have explained why, but Mom cut him off and tried to explain to him why we eat some things instead of others.

Gemma's home ec class, meanwhile, didn't have to go out in all kinds of weather and pick bugs. Her class was growing carrots. The fifth grade was making the yogurt, which had already been culturing (that's what yogurt does on the way from milk, it gets a lot of special bacteria in it and "cultures") for a couple of weeks already in a huge vat in the home ec kitchen. You could smell it, if you thought about it. A sour-bitter smell that was the strongest in the central part of the school.

Another class was fermenting tofu to make the soy-burgers out of, and that had an aroma all its own, but you had to be right on top of it to smell it.

Gemma came out to the field after her music lesson and rooted for the Marsdentown Bruins against the Sewanaka Thunderbolts. In real life, a bear is no match for a thunderbolt, but we won anyway. I got two hits, but I made an error at third base. I still had a little trouble going to my left. I told Gemma I'd ask coach to give me some extra practice at that.

"I know what you mean," she said. "When I play

the piano, my left hand's not as good as it should be, either.''

''You'll be fine,'' I said. ''Your left hand's okay when you play the flute, and when you play the guitar, right?''

''So?''

''So, your left hand's not stupid. It'll catch on.''

She looked at me. ''Jon, sometimes I don't know whether you're a bigger genius than your brother is, or just crazy.''

I grunted. ''You can ask my teachers about the genius part. But if you want to talk about somebody crazy, how about Mr. Calstone. It was like somebody gave old Homer a brain transplant.''

''I've been thinking about that,'' Gemma said. ''How was he acting today?''

''You were there. You saw him. He was acting weird. He was acting . . . *nice.*''

''In other words,'' she said, ''he was acting exactly the way all the kids who ever went to Marsdentown School since it was built in the 1960s have *wished* he would act.''

''I don't think he's actually been there since it was built. He's not old enough.''

''You know what I mean.''

''Mrs. Simpkins, on the other hand—''

''Jon, shut up and listen, okay? We have a grumpy assistant principal, we wish for a nice assistant principal, all of a sudden we've got a nice assistant principal.''

''What do you mean, 'all of a sudden'? You just pointed out kids have been wishing for that since he first showed his face.''

''Yes, but you and Michael and I were on our way

22

to meet him, and I don't know about you, but *I* was wishing he was different."

"Maybe he just decided to change," I said. "Maybe after being irritated by kids for however many years it's been, he decided to try treating them nice to see if the irritation would go down."

"Why?"

"Why not?"

"Well, look. We both wished we could have a chance to talk about the clock going crazy, and before you know it, Mrs. Simpkins sends us *both* to Mr. Calstone's office. Did you notice none of the other teachers sent anybody, let alone two kids?"

"Mrs. Zoconty sent Michael," I pointed out.

"Sure," Gemma countered. "She sent him right after we wished we could talk to him. She sent him just as we were passing by his class door."

Things like that spook me. I decided to test Gemma's theory by wishing she'd talk about something else.

"We've got to face it, Jon, something weird is going on at the school."

"Didn't work," I muttered.

"What?"

"Never mind. If something weird is going on, it doesn't sound too bad for me. We make wishes and we get them. I'll wish for a cure for disease, world peace and a million dollars."

Gemma laughed in spite of herself. "Hah!" she said. "I'm more selfish than you are. I'd just wish I could win the flute event at the County Music Competition next month."

So we started talking about that, and how winning something like that, even in seventh grade, could help her get a scholarship to college later on, and wasn't it

23

weird to be worried about college already, and other things.

I wondered if I was getting my wish, now. I pushed the thought away.

Soon, we turned into my block. You have to pass my house on the way to Gemma's. I asked her if she wanted to come in for awhile.

"Sure," she said. "Just let me call home and see if it's okay."

Gemma got clearance from her father to stay for awhile, and Mom agreed to drive her home when the time came, so that was all right. We played some ping pong in the basement while Michael did equations upstairs. In about half an hour, he joined us carrying a tray of cookies and milk Mom had put together for us. I held my breath all the time he was coming down the stairs—you'd think a genius would have realized by now that when you're carrying stuff like that, it makes a lot more sense to let your arms and legs stay fairly loose, to take up any shock that might bounce the glasses around and make them spill. Michael, though, still carries things all stiff, like Frankenstein's monster.

Fortunately, Mom had allowed for that, and had only filled the glasses up about two thirds of the way, so he made it down to us without mishap.

We nibbled cookies and sipped milk. A famous lady once said she could have stayed home and made cookies, but she became a lawyer instead. Maybe so, but our mom is great at both. These particular cookies were oatmeal raisin, and they were about the only way you could get Gemma to eat oatmeal.

After about a cookie and a half each, Michael said, "What so you think about what happened today, guys?"

We told him Gemma's wish theory.

Michael's face lit up. "That would be *cool*. Cartoons *all day* Saturday, not just in the mornings. Hamburgers every night. Trips to Mars."

I looked at him being such a kid about things, and I thought that if I believed in this wish thing, I'd wish that Dad could come back, just for a weekend, and get a load of his younger son. Michael was just a baby when Dad died, but from what I remember, they're a lot alike.

Gemma was not as amused. She stopped with a cookie in mid-dunk and said, "You don't seem to be taking this seriously."

Michael looked surprised. "I didn't know I was supposed to," he said. "Coincidences. Sometimes things work out the way you want them to. When that happens, you can *say* your wish came through, and in a way, it does. But the wish doesn't have anything to do with how things work out."

"Maybe," I speculated, "Mr. Calstone won a lottery or something, and he's going to retire, so he doesn't care anymore."

"Now there's a wish," Michael said, and we laughed. "But I was talking about the clock," he said. "The clock and the bells."

"What's to think about?" Gemma said. "They went kablooie for awhile, then they stopped. My mom would probably understand what happened; she fixes all the typewriters and printers at the shop. You guys probably understand, too."

"I wish I did," Michael said.

I tapped him on the shoulder and said "*Bing!*" Your wish has come true."

Gemma sniffed and put her nose in the air.

"Were I not eating this cookie," she said, "I would

25

come over there and thrash you both. Are you not aware that Gemma, Countess of Davis, must not be mocked?'' But she couldn't keep it up, and got the giggles. Milk didn't actually come out of her nose, but it was close.

When we were finished laughing, or at least back under control, I said to Michael, ''In Mr. Calstone's office today, you were talking about a power surge—''

''With reversed polarity, don't forget.''

''Polarity?'' Gemma said.

Michael was all set to go off and get some graph paper and colored pencils to draw her a diagram explaining polarity, but that could take all night.

''It has to do with the direction the electricity flows in,'' I said, and she was happy with that. Good thing, too, because that was about all I knew on the subject.

I turned to Michael. ''The power surge with reversed polarity sounds pretty good to me.''

''It's fine, as far as it goes,'' Michael said. ''The trouble is, where did it come from? If something like that happened in the circuits, the whole school would be messed up, probably the whole neighborhood. But it wasn't. Miss Zoconty was showing us a video about saving the spotted owl when the bell rang and the clock went nuts, and the video never even skipped a frame.''

''So if it was a power surge, it didn't come over a wire.''

''That's right,'' Michael said. ''It would have to be beamed somehow. And I don't know of anything on earth that could do that.''

''On *earth*,'' Gemma said, and we all felt a little cold.

3 Of course, once you start looking for weird things you're bound to find them, but over the next few days, we turned up a bumper crop.

It all started the next morning. Rain was pouring down as Mom drove us to school. She drives us every day, since Michael and I were thrown off the bus. Well, we weren't exactly thrown off. See, Michael can't help himself when it comes to thinking about things, and he's too young to understand why he shouldn't say everything he thinks. So, when day after day, he kept sharing his research on how dangerous schoolbuses are in accidents, especially without seatbelts for the kids, he got on everybody's nerves, and they talked to Mom about it. Mom got mad, and rearranged her schedule so she could drive us to school.

(P.S.—She also got the school board to put seat belts on the bus, but by this time we were all in the habit of her driving us, so we didn't go back.)

That Thursday morning, she dropped us off outside the main entrance, kissed us goodbye, reminded us to take our books, and drove off, promising to see us that evening.

There's a short walkway from the curb to the entrance of the school, maybe twenty yards, but in those twenty yards, I had to steer my brother away from four puddles that he would have tromped through if left on his own.

The first thing we saw inside the door was Mr. Lije. Mr. Lije is the head school custodian, a tall, skinny man with pink skin, gray hair, and a big mustache that puffs out when he talks. He always wears a little black bow tie with his gray work clothes, and he always has a smile and a hello for all the kids.

Except today. Today, he was flinging his mop at the floor of the main hallway as if he hated it.

"Good morning, Mr. Lije," Michael said.

"Yeah, yeah, good morning," he grumbled. He went on grumbling. "Bad enough they have to stink up the place with that sickly glop, so they have to track it all over the halls? Huh? More work for old Lije, that's all. Nobody knows nothing except *I'm* the one who's gotta mop it up, *humph!*"

He was still going on that way when we passed out of earshot. It was as if he and Mr. Calstone had undergone a personality swap.

I wondered how the yogurt had gotten spilled out here in the hallway, and who'd done it, and when.

I was still wondering when Michael spoke up.

"I *like* yogurt," he said.

"Me, too, especially peach. What brought that up?"

" 'Sickly glop,' " he quoted. "I don't think it's sickly glop."

"You haven't seen that tank in the home ec room. And you have to admit, he was right about stinking up the place."

Michael considered seriously, sniffed, and delivered his judgment. "Pee yew," he said.

"Exactly. I like steak, but I wouldn't want to personally kill a cow. I like yogurt, but I never knew you had to go through this smell to get it. Heck, I even like green beans, and I'll keep eating them, but I've got to tell you, I'm going to be seeing worm footprints on them for a long time to come."

"Yucko," Michael said.

I dropped him off at Miss Zoconty's room, then went on to my own homeroom. I was cheered up by the fact that the rain would a) water the green beans, and b) keep the worms at bay. First period was English; that went fine. Then strange things started happening second period, in gym class.

In the eighth grade, gym class is last period of the day, which is the best way to do it, it seems to me. In seventh grade, we have it in the morning, so we have to be sweaty on Tuesdays and Thursdays for the whole rest of the day.

When I got to the locker room, Abdul was having a fit. He was standing in front of his locker in his shorts and T-shirt and socks, holding a sneaker in his hand.

"All right, you guys," he demanded. "Who's got my other sneaker? I want it back, and I want it now."

I was glad I didn't have it. Abdul is a nice kid, which is a good thing, because he's also the biggest and strongest kid in the seventh grade.

Abdul's real name is Miles Jackson, Jr. He hated it when people called him "Junior," which most of us did through grade school because we'd heard his mother, the school secretary, call him that. Unfortunately, he didn't like the name "Miles" either. Then he found out that "Miles" means "soldier," and he liked that. Before he came to Marsdentown to become chief of police, Abdul's father had been a colonel in the Army over in Germany. Abdul was born there. It turned out that "Abdul" means soldier, just as "Miles" does, only in Arabic instead of Latin.

So he told us to call him that, and we did, because we all thought Abdul Jackson was a very cool name. Even the teachers call him that, now. His mother still calls him "Junior."

I wondered who would be stupid enough to steal a sneaker from a big, strong kid whose father was the chief of police. I decided nobody would be. I thought I'd help him track it down.

"Abdul," I said. "Where did you find the sneaker you've got?"

"What? Oh, hi, Jon. It was in my locker, with the rest of my stuff."

"You sure you put them both in the locker last time?"

"Of course I'm sure."

This didn't sound like an accidental loss. It also looked like a definite prank rather than a serious theft. The only reason I could think of to steal one sneaker is to get somebody irritated.

"Abdul, did you leave your combination on the last number?" There are three digits in the combinations on the lockers. A lot of kids leave the locker so they only have to spin the last number to get in. This defeats the whole purpose of the locker, since all anybody has to do is turn the dial slowly and try every number, but kids always do it anyway.

Abdul looked sheepish. "Don't let my pop hear about this, okay?"

Every year, Chief Jackson comes and talks to us about

security stuff. The locker business is one of the top things on his list.

"He won't hear about it from me," I said.

"What happened?"

"I was the first one down here. I was kind of running, because I had to go to the bathroom, you know? And I couldn't go to the one near English class, because Mr. Lije was in there cleaning it, splashing disinfectant around, stuff like that."

"Was there anybody here when you got here?"

"I didn't see anybody."

"How about when you got out of the bathroom?"

"Not then, either." He gave me a look. "You're starting to sound like my father."

"I'm sorry," I said. "Just trying to help."

Abdul waved off my apology. "I'm not mad, I just thought it was funny. Actually, you're helping me think. I don't see how anybody could have done it this morning. The third graders have gym first period, and they don't even come in here. And we had the place for last night's game."

"I can't see anybody staying overnight in the school just to steal one sneaker, can you?"

Abdul thought it over for a few seconds. "No," he said. "I can't." He shook his head. "I guess I must have just left it out, but I could swear I'd put them both in there."

"If you left it out, Coach probably has it in the gym office."

He had it, as we found out a few seconds later. He had it, in fact, on the floor of his own shower, sitting on an old newspaper. Coach Winoski is a short, barrel-chested guy with a crew cut he must have kept since he was in the Marines. He has a gruff manner, but from the things he says and does, you can tell he hasn't totally forgotten what being a kid is like. He'd probably make a good assistant principal someday.

"Coach," Abdul said, "how come my sneaker is in the shower?"

"It's soaking wet, Jackson. That's what happens when you leave them in the locker room sink."

"But I didn't *leave* it in the sink," Abdul said.

"Somebody did. That's where I found it when I showed up for work this morning. I should have left it for you to find, but I figured this might be a rotten prank somebody is playing on you."

"Yeah," Abdul said. "That's just what it is, and when I catch him, I'm going to—"

"You're going to tell me, and I'm going to enforce proper school discipline. That's what you meant to say, isn't it, Jackson?"

"Ah, yes, Coach."

"What else?" I said.

"What are you doing here, Parlo? If you lost a sneaker, too, you're out of luck. Jackson's is the only one I found."

"No, Coach," I said. "I was just helping Abdul look for it."

"Well, it's found now. I've got paper towels inside of it—it'll be dry in a couple of days. A little stiff, but you can break it in again."

"Thanks, Coach," Abdul said.

"Forget it," Coach Winoski told him. "Parlo, go get dressed. Jackson, let's see if I've got a pair to fit you in my sneaker bank over here."

As I went back to my own locker and got into my gym suit, I wondered if I was making mysteries where none really existed. Abdul had left his sneaker out, and somebody had come along and thrown it into the sink. People do things without remembering them all the time.

I got dressed and went over to the gym. It was set up for volleyball today, which I liked. I'd play volleyball rather than basketball in the winter time if our school had a boys volleyball team.

Abdul showed up only a few minutes late. He was wearing these amazingly strange old sneakers, made of faded red canvas, with little ventilation holes on the side. He got teased about them. He didn't say anything, but looking at his face, I could see he was making more plans for what he would do to the person who soaked his sneaker, and I don't think many of them started with telling Coach Winoski about it.

I caught up with Gemma at lunchtime, but there was no peacefulness as we joined the gang at our usual table. Abdul was still upset about gym; and it turned out that Stacy Levenson had had the reed stolen out of her clarinet in the band room.

"All right, all right," Gemma said. "Whoever it was didn't take any new reeds, just the one you'd been blowing on for the last two weeks. You'd have to change it soon, anyway."

Stacy and Gemma are friends, but they're the kind of friends who get on each other's nerves a lot, or at least act as if they do.

Now, Stacy's pink face got red, and she flounced her curly blond hair.

"It's all right for *you,* Gemma Davis. You play the *flute.* The flute doesn't have a *reed* in it that you have to pay for from your *allowance.*"

"I'll buy you a package of reeds," Gemma said with a sweet smile. "Just you, though. The whole woodwind section got the reeds plucked out of their instruments."

"Except for *you*," Stacy said. "Why would *you* offer to buy me reeds if *you* didn't have something to do with taking them?"

"Trying to make a friend feel better," Gemma said. "But forget it. It's an *orchestra*, remember? What's supposed to happen? My flute and I should make up the whole section? Give me a break, Stacy."

The rest of the meal was eaten more or less in silence. People were mentally taking sides in this Gemma-Stacy thing. New suspicions were growing about the Great Abdul Sneaker Caper.

I didn't like this. I didn't like it at all. It wasn't that these things seemed so spooky, like the bells and clocks and wishes and personality changes Mr. Calstone had been through. Missing reeds and misplaced sneakers could easily be explained away as childish pranks.

But these pranks were starting to undermine the best thing about the school—how well we got along with each other.

Like I say, I'm pretty good at history. I like it. I've read way past the textbook, and I've learned that one of the classic techniques for conquering a group of people is to get them fighting among themselves, first. It's called "Divide and Conquer."

Could the Twisters have learned enough about the human race to be able to try that tactic now?

I got Gemma away from the table, and went over into the part of the cafeteria we called Kiddieland to find my brother. Michael was engaged in a heated game of Dots with his friend, Max, the only kid his age in the school within screaming distance of Michael's intelligence.

We took a couple of teeny-little second grader seats and waited more or less patiently—Gemma more, me less. Finally, Michael eked out a close win over his friend, then asked us what we wanted.

"Your brother wants to talk, squirt."

"Council of War," I said.

Michael's face got even more serious than usual. From the time he was less than two, Michael has imagined all sorts of conquest and bloodshed. I remember the day after we first let him try to cut his own meat, he was sitting at the table sawing away, yelling, *"Death! Death by the Mighty Blade of Zanzar!"* I know Mom and I should have made him stop, but it's hard to do that when you're cracking up laughing.

It took a while, but we finally figured out how to penetrate the fantasyland. We'd call a Council of War, and explain how he was hurting his imaginary cause by these outbursts. That sort of evolved over the years to mean something Mom or I really want him to listen to.

Michael picked up his books (Professor Heimrich sends him books; he reads them in odd moments at school) and headed with us to a vacant table near the door of the kitchen where nobody likes to sit. If it was the school's other kitchen, the home ec kitchen, with the yogurt culturing away in it, for sure nobody would be sitting there.

Anyway, we sat down, and I told them my thought about Divide and Conquer.

Gemma was skeptical. "You got that from that little thing with Stacy and me? We do that all the time. We'll be all made-up again by the end of the day."

I put my face in my hands. "I almost wish we could find a monster," I said.

"Why?" Gemma demanded. "You like running for you life? You like getting stepped on by dinosaurs?"

"I like knowing what I'm up against," I said. "Heck,

35

I'd like to know if we're up against *anything*. Maybe we're just paranoid.''

"Well," Michael said. "Don't count on seeing any monsters."

"How come," I asked.

"Because we smashed up so much of the Twisters' energy gathering equipment. It takes a lot of power to do a space warp. I doubt they could send anything much bigger than a bumblebee at this point."

"Well," Gemma said. "At least nobody's been stung."

"Ha, ha. Don't you feel that there's something wrong with this school, lately?"

"Sure I do," she said. "But I'm mature enough to know that having been through what we've been through, we might be making menaces in our imaginations out of accidents and pranks."

"I *know* that," I said helplessly. "I wish I could be sure."

"Well, that's one thing," Michael said.

"What's that?"

"The wish business doesn't work anymore, if it ever did. I'll bet all three of us have been wishing that all week."

We nodded solemnly.

"I wish we could get some *help*," Gemma said.

"I wish we had the old Mr. Calstone back," Michael said.

Gemma and I were too shocked to speak. We just sat and looked at him.

"No, I mean it. In the old days, he was a pain in the neck, but if weird things like this had happened, he'd turn the school upside down to find out what was going on. He'd call an assembly and grill kids in front of everybody. He'd do *something,* that's for sure.''

Once again, the genius was right.

We sat there in gloom until the next bell rang—on time, just the way it should have. I thought of approaching Mr. Calstone anyway. Not with any alien stories or anything (I'd learned about that the hard way) but with my concerns about the pranks going on in the school. Maybe I could kindle a spark of the old grouch somewhere.

Then, on the way out of the cafeteria, Michael dropped his big science book from Professor Heimrich, something he does a lot, with the books so heavy and him so small. I turned around to pick it up for him, and found myself looking into the smiling face of Mr. Homer Calstone. He handed the book to Michael and said, ''Hey, son''—*son,* now!—''you wouldn't want to leave this.'' Then he told us to have a nice day.

All that was bad enough, but the worst was his neck. It was more surprising than vampire marks. For probably the first time since he started to dress himself, *Mr. Calstone was not wearing a tie*.

I knew then it was hopeless.

Thursday was only the start of the dreaded Marsdentown School Crime Wave. Or prank wave, or weird wave or whatever you want to call it.

On Friday, and through the next week, small, but strange and nasty things continued to happen.

- ITEM—Somebody smashed a bunch of petri dishes in the biology lab, where an eighth grader was growing bacterial cultures for a science project.
- ITEM—Mr. Lije reported that someone had emptied and wiped out the dumpster in the back of the school two days before the scheduled pickup, then had loaded all the garbage back in again.
- ITEM—More sneakers disappeared from gym lockers, including Stacy Levenson's *and* Gemma's.
- ITEM—Mrs. Jackson reported (I heard this one from Abdul) that someone had gone through her file of letters that had to be answered, and had stolen all the used envelopes, but left the letters in the file, although not in the order they'd been in. According to Abdul, his father was all set to step in and inves-

tigate, but Mrs. Vanling wouldn't hear of it. Personally, I figured Mrs. Vanling was just being touchy because her ecology idea was turning out to be a mess, because that yogurt was now stinking up the whole school.

The smell was the worst on Monday, because we'd had the weekend to get over being used to it. It had actually been a fun weekend. Abdul and Gemma came over to help me work on going to my left in baseball, and Mom took us to the mall in Booneville for lunch. We had to go there anyway, because Michael needed a new sleeping bag for the Astronomy camp out next Wednesday night.

The Astronomy camp out was a Marsdentown School tradition even older than the Spring Festival. Mr. Hungerford, who ran the observatory at State U., lives in Marsdentown, and on a June night toward the end of the school year, he invites the kids to pitch their tents on the football field and bring sleeping bags and cold food.

The cold food was important, because when you're looking at the stars, you can't start a fire to cook with, or the light from it will drown out the stars.

Mr. Hungerford sets up a big, seven-inch reflector telescope, and takes the kids on what he calls a ''guided tour of the universe,'' and what I call a really neat look at a bunch of stars and planets.

Usually, the camp out is on a Friday or Saturday night, so there'd be no school the next day, but Mr. Hungerford had arranged it this year on a Wednesday because there was a meteor shower due that he thought we ought to have a chance to see. A lot of parents and teachers who would have some pretty

39

sleepy kids on their hands the next day weren't thrilled about it, but when they were convinced this was a once in a lifetime experience, they said okay. Also, Wednesday night was the night of the new moon, so there'd be no moonlight to drown out the light from the planets and stars.

Wednesday turned out to be a great day for it, too. Michael was ready to bring his sleeping bag to school with him, but Mom explained that we'd come home, have dinner, get sandwiches and Thermoses for overnight, and then she'd drive us back to the school.

I knew the reason Michael was so eager to get there had nothing to do with the stars. He'd come into my room the night before and said, "Jon, I've been thinking about all the thefts and pranks and things."

"Yeah? So have I. I hope you've been better at it than I have."

"Jon, these things are being done overnight. There's no way a kid, or even a teacher could do *all* these things during school hours without getting caught."

"Yeah," I said. "And you know what's been bothering me? When a kid does stupid vandalism things, he always talks about it to *somebody,* even if it's only the other jerks who think it's cool to mess people up or break things. And then they talk, and word gets out sooner or later."

Michael was honestly puzzled. He's not too swift on things that aren't based on logic, unless he's seen them with his own eyes. As smart as he is, sometimes even I can forget that he's just a little kid without a lot of experience with bad people.

"Why would they do that?" he asked.

"Why would they do rotten things in the first place? Michael, some people are just jerks."

40

I changed the subject. "Michael? You say the things are being done at night. The only people in the school after the teachers go are Mr. Lije and the rest of the custodians."

"I know that."

"Why would *they* be making messes they had to clean up themselves the next morning? Their salaries are set by law. They get their raises every year—they can't blackmail the school into paying them more no matter what they do." I knew all this because Mom had been involved in the negotiations when they got their latest contract.

Michael looked at me.

"You have a nasty mind, Jon. People would really mess up their jobs to get more money? Sheesh!"

He shrugged that off. "Anyway, I'm not accusing Mr. Lije or any of the custodians. I think maybe somebody is breaking into the school."

"I'd like to think that," I said.

"Why?"

"Because then I'd know it wasn't the Twisters. But if somebody was breaking into the school, and time after time at that, wouldn't there be broken doors or windows or something?"

"Not if they had a key."

"Where would they get a key?"

"Mrs. Vanling's office," Michael said. "She keeps them in her desk drawer, all jumbled up."

"And this person, whoever it was, just strolled into Mrs. Vanling's office, reached into her drawer, and grabbed a key?"

"It wouldn't be hard," Michael said. He reached into the pocket of his robe and pulled out something shiny. "That's how I got this one."

I bounced up and snatched it out of his hand. It was a key, all right, a big, complicated one. A manilla tag was attached to it with a piece of wire; the tag said EAST DOOR.

Instinctively, I dropped my voice so Mom wouldn't hear. "Michael, are you *crazy?* Tomorrow, you go back to Mrs. Vanling's office and put this back!"

"Of course, Jon."

I breathed a sigh of relief.

"I'm gong to put it back tomorrow night, after we sneak away from the camp out and search the school for whoever's doing these crazy things. I'll drop it off back in Mrs. Vanling's office before we leave."

I was about to tell him he would do no such thing, that he would do it as early in the day as he could manage, what was he, nuts? Did he want to get expelled? More importantly, did he want *me* to get expelled? *He* was a genius; he didn't really need school, in a way. He'd already taught himself more than most people get around to learning. But I'm just a regular guy, and if I get a bad record, it can hurt me for years, not to mention that it will humiliate Mom.

But then my fear took over, and the thought that I could be sure that the Twisters weren't doing this was so tempting . . .

I know it was wrong. I knew it then, actually.

"All right, Michael," I said at last. "I'll go along with you on this."

"I thought you would."

"Don't be so smug. If we get caught, I almost think I'd rather be back with the Twisters."

"You don't mean that."

"Of course not. But it won't be fun if we do, little brother. We might even get blamed for what's happened

42

so far, ever think of that? Calstone would finally have the excuse he needed to ship you off to Princeton.''

Michael grinned. ''That's the *old* Mr. Calstone.''

''He may return at any moment.''

''Maybe. But Jon, look on the bright side. If we catch whoever's doing it, we can turn them in. They'll be so happy to have the mess stopped, they'll probably throw us a party.''

''You watch too many cartoons,'' I said.

''Don't worry, Jon. You'll see.''

''That's what I'm afraid of,'' I said.

5

I put my face to the eyepiece of the telescope and looked at the sky. I was supposed to be looking at the Crab Nebula, but I was paying just as much attention to the stars around it.

Any one of those, I thought, could be the original home of the Twisters. Or none of them could be. The universe was just *so big*. And we couldn't even be sure if they were from this universe.

I didn't really want to be doing this, you see. Once we'd decided to stake out the school tonight, I wanted to go and do it. Gemma, though, said we had to arrange things so that we wouldn't be missed. Yes, Gemma was coming with us. She deserved the shot, having been in on the adventures from the beginning, but as usual, the real reason was that she was so good at handling grownups, I wanted her to deal with things if we got in trouble.

She was dealing with it, now. The idea was for each of us to make an appearance at the telescope before we sneaked off to the school building, and again after.

I was the last one to go. When I figured I'd looked long enough at the sky, then oohed and ahhed over a few meteors, I went and found Gemma, who was talking to her mother, one of the chaperones for the night.

"Time?" I asked.

"Time," she agreed. "You go get Michael, I'll tell Stacy to cover for me"—they were sharing a tent—"and you're next door to who?"

"To whom," I corrected automatically.

"Yes, Jon, thank you. That's very important right now. Whom is your tent next to?"

That time, it should have been "who." She never can get that right, but I let it go. "Abdul and Biff," I said.

"Good. They'll cover for you, won't they?"

"Sure they will."

I found Michael talking with Abdul and his tentmate for the evening, Biff Elkins. Biff *looks* like he ought to be named Biff. He's blond and broad and muscular. He's our star pitcher. He's not too interested in school work, but the rest of the guys on the team ride his butt to study so he stays eligible to play. It says a lot for Biff that he stops complaining every couple of weeks to thank us for it, usually after he pitches a good game and wins.

Gemma was waiting for us at the east goal post, down the other end of the football field from the telescope. It was just about thirty yards from there to the door Michael had taken the key to. We went carefully, one at a time, dashing from shrub to shrub until we made it.

"Michael," I said. "Give me the key."

He made his thundercloud face. "Why?"

"Because if anybody catches us while we're in the act of opening the door, you two can run and I'll take the rap."

"Don't be ridiculous," Gemma said. "The squirt is

45

a seven-year-old genius. Let him do it, and *we* can run. He can claim he's just being eccentric.''

''Gemma, you're probably right,'' I said. ''But do you honestly think I could run away and leave my baby brother? Or my best friend?''

She put a finger to her chin and looked at me closely. ''No, Jon, I don't think you could.'' Then she grinned and batted her eyelashes at me. ''That must be why I love you so.''

''Don't be disgusting,'' I said.

Gemma and Michael's laughter could probably be heard at the Crab Nebula.

''*Quiet!*'' I snapped.

They shut up. Michael gave me the key. I turned it and pulled the door open.

A school is a spooky place at night. The familiar hallways, lit only with the service lights, are filled with weird shadows that are never there in the daytime. Footsteps that are usually lost in the general bustle of the day echo off the walls. Even your breath sounds horribly loud. Teachers are always yelling at kids for silence, but if they had to spend all day in a silence like this, they'd be happy for a little noise.

That was the first thing I noticed. The second thing was the smell. I wasn't alone in that.

''Geez,'' Gemma said. ''While we're here, let's do everybody a favor and dump that yogurt down a toilet bowl.''

''It'll be delicious when it's finished and has the fruit in it.''

''Yeah, but in the meantime, wow.''

''Better not dump it in the West Wing girls' room,'' Michael said.

"How come? That's the nearest one to the home ec kitchen."

"Mr. Lije disinfected in there today. If we slop yogurt all over the place, he's going to have a fit."

"Wait a minute," I said. "I just thought of something."

"Congratulations," Gemma said. I could tell she was nervous. She always makes wisecracks when she's nervous.

"The prankster, whoever it is, has messed up all kinds of stuff, but he hasn't done anything to the yogurt. You'd thing with all the talk about it, he'd go right there, wouldn't you?"

"Maybe Mrs. Delehanty keeps the home ec room locked," Gemma suggested.

Michael said, "Locked doors haven't kept whoever it is out of the school, have they?"

"Good point."

"Let's go have a look at the home ec room," I said. "We'd have to wait for this guy somewhere, right?"

We went, on down past the center stem into the lower school wing, where the home ec room and kitchen were. We walked carefully and as quietly as we could. If there *was* someone else in here, we didn't want to alert them of our presence.

In the daytime, the school doesn't seem all that long, but that night, the corridor went on for *miles*. As we passed the offices, I was tempted to tell Michael to put the key back in Mrs. Vanling's desk, and let's just scram.

But, once again, I didn't want to look like a chicken in the eyes of my brother and my friend, so I just kept plodding along.

Michael saw it first. He froze and put his little hands out to stop Gemma and me.

47

"Look," he whispered.

We looked. The door to the home ec room was open. *Wide* open, just kind of waving on its hinges in the draft you always get in a big long hallway.

After a couple of seconds of gawking, Michael plastered himself against the wall in which the door was set like a master spy infiltrating an enemy's lair. He has a lot of spy fantasies, too.

Well, I couldn't let a seven year old lead the way into what looked like it could be a dangerous situation, so I scooted up ahead of him and plastered myself to the wall and spy-inched my way there. I looked back at one point, and saw Gemma *behind* Michael doing exactly the same thing, and I almost blew everything by laughing.

When I got to the door, I didn't feel like laughing anymore. You could sense something was wrong about the room, and not just the door being open. We went on through the classroom, and into the kitchen.

"It's gone," Gemma said. "Somebody did it."

She was pointing at the yogurt vat. The lid was leaning against a wall, as though it had been carelessly tossed there, and the ceramic tub it usually covered was empty. No yogurt, anywhere.

The smell was terrible. I held my nose when I looked over the edge.

"Nod a drace of yogurd," I said.

"What?" Gemma demanded.

I took my hand from my nose. "Not a trace of yogurt, I said."

"Somebody dumped it," Gemma said.

I wanted to go back to holding my nose, but the other two weren't bothering, so I just breathed through my mouth. "I don't know," I said. "What did Mrs. Vanling say was supposed to be in there? Thirty-two gallons of yogurt? That had to weigh . . .''

While I was trying to figure it out, Michael said, "Over five hundred pounds."

"How could anybody dump five hundred pounds of yogurt without spilling a drop?"

"Well, where *is* it then?" Gemma demanded. "How did even the Phantom of Marsdentown do this?"

Michael had a paper towel in his hand. I thought he was going to blow his nose, but instead he said, "Jon, please lift me up. I'd like to see inside the vat."

Mom has a rule that when Michael asks politely for something, we should give it to him if it's at all possible. I hefted him and held him over the rim.

"Not much to see," I said.

He swiped at the tub of the yogurt vat with the paper towel, then said thanks. I let him down.

"The heating elements are still on," he said. "There's supposed to be heat in this thing, right?"

"Yeah," Gemma said. She seemed a little surprised that there was something Michael didn't know. "It helps the bacteria culture the yogurt faster."

"Well, it's still warm. And whenever the yogurt vanished, it wasn't too long ago. Look."

He held up his piece of paper towel so we could see the wet spot where he'd wiped.

"Another mystery," Gemma grumbled, and I knew just how she felt.

We were still grumbling about it when the monstrous white form loomed up in the doorway, and we heard that bubbling roar for the first time as it tried to get us.

As we drew back from the explosion of liquid nastiness that marked the yogurt's escape from the library, a strange thing happened. It parted around us, dividing itself into two pools of mess, then quickly formed up into monsters again.

Now we were cut off in both directions, by monsters half the bulk of the single one, but just as frightening.

They began to close in on us.

"Jon?" My brother said. "Gemma?" He was using his trying-not-to-cry voice. "I'm sorry I got you into this."

"Wouldn't have missed it, squirt," Gemma said. Her voice was pretty shaky, too.

If this went on for thirty more seconds, I *would* be crying. "Can we please save the goodbyes and think of something?"

Ordinarily, Gemma would have come back with a sarcastic remark—she'd say, "Like *what*, for instance?" or something like that. This time, she was silent, and I knew she was as scared as I was.

Then she brightened. "The thing hasn't cut us off completely. Come on!"

She grabbed us both by the hand and pulled us through a solid wooden door.

Michael looked around, saw the tiles and the toilet stalls, but no urinals.

"Hey," he said, "this is the *girls' room!*"

Gemma rolled her eyes. "On behalf of the girls of America, I give you permission to be here. Jon, try to get the window open."

I had already thought of that, and had already failed. The only windows that opened at Marsdentown school were little six-inch wide panels that a good sized cat would have trouble getting through. I looked around to find something to smash the glass with, with, there was nothing loose in the place except for some empty bleach bottles in the trash can, probably left there by Mr. Lije when he disinfected the place today.

"What's the monster waiting for?" Michael wondered. "He knows we're in here. He was looking right at us, or whatever it is he does, when we came in."

"I sprayed him with something in the library, and he didn't like it. Maybe it's afraid I still have it."

I tried one of the bleach bottles, anyway. As I figured, the plastic bottle just bounced off the window pane.

"Why didn't you keep it, for crying out loud?" Gemma demanded.

"I tried to," I assured her.

I was trying even harder to break the window now, but all I was doing was flattening the plastic. I thought of picking up the whole garbage can and trying that, but that was plastic, too.

"Here it comes," Gemma said.

The door started to open. We could see the whiteness behind it.

"It's huge again," Michael said. "It merged back together."

The arm that pushed at the door oozed longer and longer as the effort went on until the door was wide open.

It slid a "foot" into the room, then the other. It started to gurgle. The "feet," which had had no trouble getting traction on any surface in the school before, seemed to go all liquid, and the creature began to slip, like a comedian in a movie hitting a banana peel.

Still, it was sliding in our direction.

I was just so mad. It wasn't fair. We were just kids; for all his brain power, Michael was still practically a baby. Why did *we* get stuck with being the ones who had to save the school, the town, the earth from disgusting monsters?

I still had my hands on the garbage can. If I'd given it a thought, I would never have done what I did—a creature capable of popping a steel lock and a solid wood door would hardly be hurt by some molded plastic, but I wasn't thinking. I just wanted to lash out.

I took a couple of quick steps, then whipped the garbage can along the clean tiles at the yogurt monster. The can skidded along the floor, and wobbled, but it never did quite tip over. Instead, it hit the creature with a *plook* and sort of stuck in the glop of its body.

The monster started to ooze around it, and I thought all I'd done was provide a sneak preview of what was going to happen to us, but after that, amazing things started to happen.

First, the garbage can came flying back at me. It was

as though the creature hadn't liked the taste of it, and had spit it out with its entire body.

Then it screamed. I don't know how a blob of bacteria-cultured skim milk can scream, but it did. Michael said it was just a simultaneous release of all the gas bubbles that form under any fermentation process, but even he admits it sounded like a scream of pain.

While it was screaming, it changed again. It drew in the false arms and legs that had made it look like a joke version of a man, got a little taller and a lot more cylindrical, then grew the characteristic tentacles that made up the unmistakable shape of the Twisters.

Now we know, I thought, as we gawked at the form we saw in our nightmares.

It only stayed in Twister shape for a few seconds. Then it merged the tentacles back into its body, put out ''arms'' and ''legs'' and a lump of ''head.''

Then it ran.

And for a change, it ran *away* from us.

I went to the door of the room, looked out, and saw it moving down the hall, toward the east door.

I reported this, and said, ''Let's go out the west door.''

Gemma shook her head. ''Uh uh, Jon,'' she said. ''For some reason, it can't stand this garbage can. Let's chase it right out into the ball field. Then *everybody* will see it, and we'll get the town against it.''

''Good idea,'' Michael said. He went back into the bathroom, and began stuffing things back into the can. ''We don't know exactly what it didn't like,'' he explained.

''Yeah,'' I said. Well, I thought, if I'd ever had any ideas about giving orders to these two, I'd learned better now. My heart and brain were headed to the west door and safety, but my feet went after the monster.

It was easy enough to make speed, since I didn't have to carry the garbage can, just push it along ahead of me on the slick stone tiles of the hallway.

I could hear from their footsteps that Gemma and Michael were right behind me.

"We're gaining on it," I said. "We're out of our minds, but we're gaining on it."

Then the creature did the strangest thing it had done yet. It ducked into a bathroom, the East Wing boys' room.

"Now we've got it cornered," said Michael gleefully.

I wasn't feeling glee. That creature could pop a window as easily as it popped a door (though I supposed that would achieve the purpose of getting it out in the open where it wasn't a secret anymore). Furthermore, the one thing I'd accomplished by hitting it with the garbage can at the other side of the school was to turn in into a Twister. That was fine when it decided to run away. In an enclosed space, I didn't think it was much of an improvement at all.

We stopped outside the door and listened for a moment. Then I closed my eyes, said a little prayer, took a deep breath, and said, "All right."

I gripped the garbage can. Gemma and Michael slammed their shoulders into the door, slamming it open. I took my two little running steps, but I never flung the trash. I was too busy watching what the creature was doing.

"Will you look at that," I said.

What it was doing was disappearing; oozing its way down one of the floor drains. I shouldn't have been surprised; anything that can ooze under a door can slide down a drain, but this almost looked as if the creature was committing suicide.

Michael wanted to run for a closer look, but I caught him by the back of the belt and wrapped him up in my arms until the monster was all gone. Then, cautiously, the three of us approached the drain. We got there in time to see the last of the whiteness disappearing into the depths of the school's piping with a low throaty gurgle.

"Wow," Michael said. "Did you see the Twister shape?"

"We saw it," Gemma said. She rubbed her chin. "You know, this could be a trap. He might have split before he did this."

"You have," I said, "the jolliest thoughts."

Nevertheless, pushing our trusty magic garbage can ahead of us, we searched the school—twice—and found nothing. At last, we were able to leave.

Just outside the east door, Michael said, "Mrs. Vanling is going to be mad."

"Why?"

"No yogurt for the spring festival."

7

Things were pretty quiet when we got back to the camp out. A lot of the younger kids were asleep, and people were wandering up to the telescope only one or two at a time.

We put in our return appearance with Mr. Hungerford, still shaken by what happened at school, and still frustrated by the knowledge that we didn't have proof of one darned thing.

In our absence, the stars had moved, and Mars had come into view, as well. It really was red. I couldn't see any canals, but I knew they weren't really there, anyway. We didn't need to see canals on Mars to convince us that there was life on other planets.

Nobody had said anything about our being away, at least not yet. Gemma said she'd better get back to her tent before Stacy let her imagination run away with her.

"We'll talk about this tomorrow," she said.

I agreed, but what we were going to say was beyond me. I was worn out, and more confused than ever. It was possible that we had actually defeated the Twisters' yogurt monster tonight, but somehow, I just didn't believe it.

Michael yawned. When I looked down, he was rubbing his eyes and looked remarkably like a teddy bear. If I'm worn out, I thought, imagine how he must feel. I brought him back to the tent. In the next tent over, Abdul and Biff were still up, playing checkers.

"Anybody miss us?" I asked.

"You were gone?" Abdul answered.

"Droll," I said. "Seriously. Did anybody come looking for us?"

"Nope. But you were away so long, Biff snuck over and ate your sandwiches."

"I did not!" Biff said hotly.

Abdul gave what he calls his fiendish cackle. "Joke, Biff. I swear, you are so easy."

"Ha, ha," I said. At the mention of the word "sandwiches," I remembered that I was starving.

Suddenly, the guys were serious.

"Hey," Biff said. "Did you find anything?"

"Oh, boy," I began, but Michael cut me off.

"Somebody popped the lock on the library door," he said. "And somebody got rid of the yogurt."

Biff and Abdul burst out laughing. "I wish!" Biff said. "My mom is complaining that the smell is sticking to my clothes!"

"Yeah," Abdul said. "Good one, Michael."

Michael started to protest that it was the truth, but this time I cut him off.

"Well," I said, "don't be surprised. We're going to hit our tent now, guys. I need my beauty sleep."

"*That's* a lost cause," Abdul said. Even my baby brother laughed at that one.

"Anyway," I went on, "thanks for standing by."

"No problem," Biff said. "I just wish you'da got something on that creep."

"Me, too," I said.

Back in the tent, I asked Michael why he didn't level with the guys; we had said we were going to do that at the start of the evening. Gemma, who knows the infinitely more complicated rules girls use with each other, was going to decide if she told Stacy when she saw her.

"We will level with them," Michael said. "Not just yet. There's something I want to think about, but I'm too tired to think. What kind of food did Mom pack?"

I opened the cooler she'd sent. "Let's see. Ham, chicken salad, tuna. Two of each. Bunches of oranges. What did you want to think about?"

Michael finished yawning before he told me. "Why did the monster run from the girls' room and head for the boys' room?"

"Maybe they have very strict hallway monitors on the Twisters' planet."

"Oh, ha, ha. Food and sleep, Jon. What else have we got?"

I looked back in the cooler. "Chocolate milk. Two bags of potato chips." I started to laugh. "And two containers of yogurt. Strawberry and vanilla. I'll keep the lids on tight."

We were hungrier than we thought; we cleaned out that cooler. Except for the yogurt.

Then Michael said, "Oh, fooey. Give me the vanilla."

"Yeah," I said, as I took the strawberry and grabbed a couple of plastic spoons. "Why the heck not?"

Michael opened the lid on his and drew back the foil, revealing an all-too-familiar whiteness inside, but none of the sour smell. He raised his spoon high, stared at the yogurt cup, then plunged the spoon in.

"*Revenge!*" he yelled just before he plopped a big load of it in his mouth.

We were still smiling when we went to sleep.

Gemma's mother drove us home early the next morning. Mom came out to the porch in her robe and slippers and invited everyone to breakfast. The moms asked if we'd enjoyed ourselves.

"It was amazing," Gemma said. Truth blazed from her green eyes.

Mrs. Davis said, "You look like me, but you take after your father. He's always going on about the wonders of the universe. All I can say is that a wonder has to be pretty darned wonderful to be worth missing a good night's sleep."

Or pretty darned horrible, I thought.

After breakfast, Gemma went home with her mom, I took a quick shower and got dressed for school, then waited for Michael.

That kid can take so long in the shower, sometimes Mom and I are afraid he's slipped down the drain.

I shuddered, remembering the whiteness of the creature disappearing down there.

Michael was still getting dressed when Mom called for us to hurry so she could drive us to school and get to the office. On the way downstairs, I asked him if he'd had a chance to do any of that thinking he'd planned to do.

"Some of it." But that was all he had the chance to say before Mom hustled us out to the car.

Gemma was waiting for us at school.

"Gee," she said. "Seems like I just left you guys."

"Michael's been thinking," I said.

"Uh oh," Gemma said. "What have you been thinking about, squirt?"

"Well, I think I know how the yogurt creature managed to slurp around the school all this time without leaving blobs of yogurt behind him. At least for the last few days. Mr. Lije hasn't been complaining lately."

"Yeah," I said. "Come to think of it, the only clue that it was here has been that smell."

Gemma shrugged. "I figured the Twisters were keeping it together with some kind of ray, or something."

Michael shook his head. "That would be sure to cause more interference with clocks and things, like the original time warp. I think the yogurt creature is held together with surface tension."

"It makes me tense enough," Gemma said.

"Come on, you know what surface tension is. Molecular charges in water molecules make it form a kind of skin at the surface. That's why you can fill a glass so that water bulges over the top of it, and why water on a car makes drops instead of just a sheet."

Gemma admitted she had known that.

"Yogurt is mostly water," Michael said. "Just like us. The creature has developed a skin of surface tension."

"Makes sense," I said. "But you know what's been bothering me? Why it did what it did. We know now the Twisters sent it; what do the Twisters hope to accomplish by stealing sneakers and clarinet reeds? Why go messing around in garbage dumpsters or breaking petri dishes?"

"Why," Michael said slowly, "did it like the dumpster, but fear the garbage can you threw at it last night? Why did it hate the girls' room and run to the boys' room?"

"You keep coming back to that," I said.

"I can't help thinking it's the key to the whole

60

thing," he said. "Look, the creature may be gone now, but this wasn't a big project for the Twisters, like trying to fill the town with dinosaurs. If they could do this once, they can do it again whenever they want, if we don't figure out what to do about it."

"I see what you mean," Gemma said. "Ordinarily, if somebody asked me what to do about a bunch of yogurt, I'd say, 'Eat it!' But I'm not eating anything that fools around in garbage bins and slides down bathroom drains. In fact—"

She stopped. Not because she'd run out of things to say, but because Michael had frozen in place as though he'd stepped on a live wire.

"Oh!" he said. "Oh! Of course."

"Of course *what?*" I demanded.

Just then, the bell rang for school to start.

"No time now," my brother said. "Jon, you have home ec today?"

"Third period. Why?"

"Check that vat. Council of War at lunchtime. Got to get to class. Got to think."

He ran off toward his class. "Did you ever think," I said to Gemma, "that it might not be too much fun to be a genius?"

"I don't know," she said. "*I* enjoy it."

"Gemma, I'm not a genius, and I'm scared. Check the vat for what?"

"I don't know, Jon," she said, serious for once. "If it makes you feel any better, I'm scared, too."

It didn't make me feel any better, but I couldn't see any use in saying so. The second bell rang, and we went in to homeroom.

In homeroom, at long last, the school admitted something was going on. There was a Very Angry Indeed speech by Mrs. Vanling over the public address system that talked about "incidents" and "petty theft" and "vandalism" (no specifics) and how it was intolerable and had to stop. She promised severe punishments for anybody who got caught doing the stuff.

I didn't worry too much about it, because I figured it was all over, at least for now. It was interesting that Mrs. Vanling did the announcing herself. That kind of thing used to be the assistant principal's department. Either the new Mr. Calstone was too big a wuss these days to be trusted with making threats, or Mrs. Vanling was so upset at the loss of her yogurt that she had to take to the intercom in person.

I sort of went sleepwalking through the first two periods. Part of it was because I was just plain tired. I'd had a strenuous night, and not as much sleep as I like to get. But most of it was that I was distracted. What had come to Michael in that last second before the bell rang. What the heck was I supposed to check the yogurt vat *for?* And why was I so uneasy?

We'd beaten the Twisters again, hadn't we? It would be a heck of a thing if I got to the point when I was happier when hostile aliens were invading earth, because at least then I wasn't worrying about the *next* time they would do it.

"*Jon!*" the teacher would say, "Please rejoin the class. You're a million miles away."

At least.

Anyway, at last it was time for home ec class. I wanted to make a beeline for the kitchen, but I was handed an apron, sent to a counter, and joined my classmates in blanching green beans.

It's a good thing caterpillars like to eat them, because if they didn't, the earth would be covered in green beans. You keep the worms away from them, and the plants will just keep making beans until you're sick of the sight of them. We got so many from just that little stand of plants outside that we had been stringing, blanching, and freezing the darn things (and picking them, of course) for a long time, now. We'd prepared enough for the dinner. There was enough left over to feed the rest of the county for a week. I had a feeling that the green beans we now had filling up the freezer were going to be on the lunch menu every single day next year.

Finally, I got transferred from stringing to blanching, boiling the beans for a short time so they'll stay green when you freeze them. To do that, I had to leave the workroom for the kitchen.

I didn't have to do anything special to check out the yogurt vat. The lid was off. There was a gaggle of kids around it, the class responsible for the yogurt. It wasn't their usual home ec period, but sometimes food won't go by the school's schedule. They weren't standing around an empty vat wondering where their dessert had gotten to. They were taking huge ladles full of the white stuff and filling pots to go in the refrigerator.

I stared in horror. I was glad that none of the kids (they were fifth graders) was tempted to taste a fingerful while they worked. The smell in here was even more intense than it had been last night. I heard one kid say he'd be glad when they got this stuff shut away in the fridge. Another said it would be all right once they got it mixed with the honey and the peaches at the dinner tomorrow night.

I was just glad their dessert-to-be didn't reach up and try to strangle them.

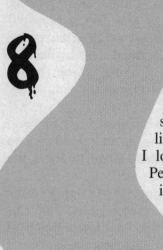

"It didn't do *anything*," I said. "It just sat there and acted like *yogurt*."

Gemma put her hand on mine for a second. "Maybe," she said, "you should try to talk a little more quietly, Jon."

I looked around the lunchroom. People were looking at me. I realized then that I had probably just said the stupidest thing any of them had ever heard.

"Okay," I said quietly. "But it was there. It was back."

Gemma narrowed her eyes at my brother, who was innocently nibbling a fish stick.

"You're not surprised, are you, squirt?" she said. "You expected this all along."

Nod aw awong," he said.

"Don't talk with your mouth full," I told him.

He chewed and swallowed. "Not all along. Just since this morning, Gemma. Since you said you didn't want to eat anything that had been down a bathroom drain."

"I still don't. I don't want anybody else to, either."

"Of course not. But I think we're going to have to do something drastic to stop them. Might get us in big trouble."

"Forget that for now," I said. "Why weren't you surprised after what Gemma said?"

"Because I remembered what makes yogurt yogurt—bacteria."

"Yeah. Acidophilous bacillus, I think they told us. So?"

"So, Jon. It explains everything. It stole sneakers and clarinet reeds and broke petri dishes to get at bacteria cultures, and it wallowed around in the dumpster and went down the boys' room floor drain."

"Right," Gemma breathed, "right. Michael, you *are* a genius. It's *been harvesting bacteria from all over the school.*"

"I get it," I said. "That's why it hated Mr. Nathans's spray I picked up in the library, and why its feet got all gooshy when it started coming into the girls' room after us. The throat spray was antiseptic, and Mr. Lije had disinfected the girls' room that very afternoon. This stuff killed the germs the yogurt was made of!"

Suddenly I frowned. "Why did it react so badly to the garbage can I threw at it? Garbage doesn't kill germs."

"Bleach does," Gemma said. "Remember, it had those empty bleach bottles in it? There must have been enough bleach left inside to hurt it badly when it tried to absorb the germs from the paper towels and stuff that were in the garbage."

Michael nodded as he crunched a carrot stick. He loves finger food. "That's why he ran away from us, after that. And since the boys' room gets disinfected on Tuesday, he didn't have to worry about using that drain—enough bacteria had built up again for it to be safe."

"You mean," I said, "after we left the school thinking we were through with it, it just oozed back up out of the drain, left the bathroom, and went back to its vat like a good little blob of yogurt.''

Michael shrugged. ''I don't know. It might have slopped around looking for more bacteria, first.''

''What does it want with all this bacteria?'' Gemma wanted to know. ''It had plenty to start with.''

Michael scowled, the way he does when he's worked on a problem and the answer hasn't come.

''I don't know,'' he said. ''The best I can figure is that when the clocks went crazy, the Twisters were creating a mini-time warp, and sent a tiny culture of that bacteria to our time. Maybe it was supposed to land on a person, and start a disease.''

''There's a happy thought,'' Gemma said.

''Or maybe,'' Michael went on, ''it was *supposed* to float along until it hit some cheese or yogurt or something like that. Anyway, I think this stuff needs other bacteria to keep going. Like, our bodies can make some proteins up from molecules, but others we've just got to get from eating. That's what vitamins are, you know— proteins our bodies can't make.''

''I think the yogurt creature needs more bacteria all the time to supply something it can't make for itself.''

Gemma scratched her head. ''So where did the Twisters get this amazing bacteria? From their home planet?''

''It could be as simple as that,'' Michael said. ''Maybe all they had to do was sneeze into a tissue— or whatever it is a Twister might do—to get the bacteria. But I don't think so. I think they genetically engineered it. We've seen their science. They can do lots of things we won't be able to do for years.''

''No,'' I said.

''Why not, Jon?'' Gemma asked. ''I hate to admit it,

but the squirt is making sense. Why shouldn't it be genetically engineered?''

''I didn't mean it wasn't genetically engineered. Now that you mention it, Michael, I think it probably is.''

''What's the problem, then?''

''It thinks. You can genetically engineer until you're inside out, but I don't think even the Twisters can genetically engineer a germ that thinks. This stuff doesn't just react when things happen. Those fifth graders were doing a lot worse to it than we did, but it just sat there. That's why I was so loud about it when you asked what it was doing when I saw it. It couldn't gain anything from acting up in front of so many people, so it didn't.''

''I see what you mean,'' Gemma said. ''So how are they doing it?''

We both looked at Michael.

''Got me,'' he said. ''I'll think about it.''

''I just have the feeling,'' I said, ''that if we could figure out what it—and the Twisters—were trying to do, we'd have a better chance of stopping it.''

''What do you mean, what it's trying to do?''

''I've said this before. We know that the Twisters want the town emptied out for a couple of days to build their war machines, right?''

''Right,'' Gemma said. ''They told us that when they had us captured in the past.''

''All right, then. They get this creature roaming around, creating mischief, causing suspicion among kids and teachers in the school. It's not nice, but it's not going to empty out the town, either. There must be something more to their plan, something horrible, and we've got to figure it out.''

Gemma pursed her lips, and thought. ''Well,'' she

67

said at last, "I can't figure out what the creature is going to do, but I bet I know when it's going to do it."

"When?" I asked.

"If it wants to empty out the town—"

"Or kill us all off," I added.

Gemma nodded grimly. "Or that," she continued, "its best chance will be at the banquet tomorrow night. Half the town is going to be there, all the school-age kids and their parents. We'll all be under one roof. Heck, we'll all be in the same room. Mr. Lije and his staff are setting up tables in the gym even now."

That was new this year. The banquet of the Spring Festival had previously been held in the cafeteria, but last year it had been so crowded, you couldn't lift your fork to eat without poking somebody.

Right now, Michael, who had been oddly quiet, put his carrot stick down and stared at something very far away.

Gemma noticed him first.

"Look at him," she said. "Hey, squirt, don't go having fits on us, now."

Quietly, I said, "What is it, Michael?"

He whispered something so low I didn't get it.

"What's that?" I asked.

Now he practically screamed it. "Disease, Jon! Disease!"

"Now people are looking at you, champ," I told him. "They're going to think we're both nuts. Calm down and explain."

He calmed down, a little. At least he lowered his voice.

"I don't want anybody," he said, "to call me a genius ever again, okay? I'm a dope. I should have thought of this as soon as this business started."

"Well, squirt," Gemma said, "whatever it is, Jon and I still haven't thought of it, so if you're a dope, what does that make us?"

Michael smiled in spite of himself.

"Assistant dopes," he said. Then he got serious again. "Bacteria. That's the key. Bacteria doesn't just make yogurt, it causes disease. This thing hasn't been eating dirty sneakers and clarinet reeds and experimental cultures and garbage and whatever it found in the drains just to keep up its surface tension, it's been using the genetic material of the bacteria it's found to breed a sickness."

"Oh, Lord," Gemma breathed. "A new bacteria . . ."

"Right," Michael said. "One we probably don't have any good medicines for. Pieced together from the germs we live surrounded by most of the time. We've built up some immunity to them the way they are, but recombined, who knows?"

"And a lot of disease germs are immune to us, these days, too," I said. "They always have to keep coming up with new antibiotics, because the germs evolve an immunity. I read that in one of Mom's magazines."

"That's right," Gemma said. "Once people caught this thing, scientists could probably come up with *something* to fight it, but not before our whole town was flat on its back with this new disease. That would give the Twisters easy pickings of us, and give them plenty of time to build their weapons."

"Wait a minute," I said. "This germ isn't invulnerable," I said. "It was afraid of Mr. Nathans's spray. It was afraid of the bleach."

"Sure," Michael said. "There are a lot of things that will kill any bacteria before you get it. I bet Mom has bottles of ten different things that will do it under the sink right now at home. But they don't do any good once the germ is in your body, because if you drink or inject that stuff, it will kill you just as dead as the germ will.''

"Of course," I said. "I guess I'm the dope."

Gemma was impatient. "Nobody's a dope, okay? Let's just figure out what we're going to do about this."

"That's simple," Michael said. "We've got to stop anybody from eating that yogurt, no matter what."

"How are we going to do that?" I asked.

"I said it was simple," Michael said gloomily. "Not easy."

With that, the bell rang, and we had to split up.

I didn't see Gemma again until seventh period math class. Until about halfway through the lesson Gemma had been looking as glum as I felt. Suddenly, her face lit up with a big grin. I wondered what the heck she was so happy about. I almost wished the clocks would run backward again so we could get a chance to talk about it.

Finally, the class was over, and we met out in the hall.

"What are you so happy about?" I demanded.

"I've got it," she said.

For a panic-stricken split second I thought she meant she had the disease the Twisters' yogurt monster was brewing up.

"Got what?"

"Got the solution to our problem."

"What is it?"

"The problem is, we've been so busy trying to be heroes, we forgot to be kids. What do kids do when we're in trouble?"

"Cry? I've certainly felt like it."

"No. We get a grownup to fix it for us."

70

"Fix it? They won't even believe it."

"Look, after school, just get your brother and meet me at Mrs. Vanling's office. And let me do the talking."

We didn't get in to see Mrs. Vanling right away— she had business details to go over with Mr. Calstone. While the school emptied, we overheard them talking about the budget for chalk, what to do about snow days next year, end-of-the-year gifts for the office staff— dozens of things you'd never think about when you thought about what it would take to run a school. To every question the principal raised, Mr. Calstone responded with a cheery, "No problem I'll handle it." I wondered how he'd handle this. I was still wondering how Gemma was going to handle it.

Michael was sitting between Gemma and me, swinging his legs the way little kids do when they're impatient. Mom would have made him stop. I just sat there quietly going bonkers from the suspense.

Finally, they were done, and Mr. Calstone came and opened the door and asked us in. He stood behind Mrs. Vanling while we talked to her.

Mrs. Vanling has kind of a big nose, but she's a neat looking lady all the same. She has nice blue eyes (unless she's mad, then they're not nice at all), and smooth blond hair with a couple of streaks of silver in it.

Even though she had a lot on her mind, she found a smile for us. "Hello, children. What can I do for you."

Gemma tilted her head sideways, in that woman-to-woman way I've seen my mother use in court. Oprah Winfrey does it, too.

"Mrs. Vanling," she said. "I know this will be a lot of trouble, but I think you should consider not serving the yogurt tomorrow night."

"Now Gemma, I know the smell has been hard to

put up with''—her smile got wider—''and worse than I anticipated, but when it's prepared as a dessert, it will be fine.''

''See, ma'am, we're not sure of that.''

Talk about an understatement.

''What do you mean, Gemma?'' Mr. Calstone put in.

''All the ... mischief that's been going on around the school.''

Mrs. Vanling tightened her lips. ''That's a very mild word for it.''

''Yes, ma'am. The thing is, it occurred to us that if this person got inside lockers and the band room and the bio lab and all the rest, to make trouble, he or she could certainly have gotten into the home ec kitchen, and maybe done something bad to the yogurt.''

The blue eyes narrowed. ''Do you know something, Gemma?''

Gemma was all innocence. ''Not about somebody doing something to the yogurt, Mrs. Vanling.''

That was the truth. Not somebody.

''It was just,'' Gemma went on, ''something we thought of, and how it could ruin the banquet.''

''The fifth graders have worked very hard on that yogurt,'' Mr. Calstone said.

Mrs. Vanling ignored him. She was frowning. It was easy to see that yogurt sabotage was something she *hadn't* thought of.

Gemma sensed an advantage and jumped on it. ''Anyway, we just wanted to bring this to your attention. Jon and Michael's mother, the lawyer, said to tell you our concerns, and that she was certain you would do the right thing, because if anybody got sick at the banquet, the school and the town could be sued for millions, and you could be sued, too. Because you know about the pranks at the school, you see.''

''Pranks,'' Mrs. Vanling said bitterly.

''Yes, ma'am. She said you could even go to jail, but I don't believe anyone would do that. Mrs. Parlo said you were a great educator and that you cared too much to let anything bad happen, so we should just listen to you.''

Then Gemma shut up and listened.

This was usually the point where Michael would get carried away with Gemma's eloquence, and blab out something of his own, but this time I think he saw my look. He was nearly bursting with held-in enthusiasm, but he did hold it in.

Mrs. Vanling frowned for awhile, then asked Mr. Calstone his opinion.

''She does make it sound serious,'' he conceded. ''Still, the fifth graders have worked so hard. And what are the chances that someone will be—''

Mrs. Vanling gently slapped her desk. ''Any chance of harming people is too great a risk to take. Mr. Calstone, I am going down to the home economics room to tell Mrs. Delehanty that we won't be serving the yogurt after all.''

Mr. Calstone smiled brightly at her. ''A good decision,'' he beamed. ''I agree completely.''

''Thank you. Children, would you like to accompany me? Jon and Michael, you can reassure your mother that I've taken the necessary steps to make sure our dinner will be safe.''

As soon as we left the office, Mrs. Vanling lowered her voice and said, ''To tell you a secret, kids, I've been pretty sick of that smell myself.''

We laughed. We let Mrs. Vanling get a little way

ahead of us, then I grinned a big grin and slapped Gemma on the back. Michael made an okay sign with his hand and whispered, "That was great!"

I whispered, too. I asked her if she'd really talked to my mother.

She nodded. "Called her right after school. I maybe exaggerated what she said a little, but it was all true."

I said, "Wait until you get her bill," and Gemma slugged me.

The home ec room was quiet as we walked in. It was so quiet, in fact, that I thought I could hear a certain telltale gurgling coming from the kitchen.

"Mrs. Delehanty?" Mrs. Vanling called.

Michael pulled at my sleeve. "Do you hear that?"

"I hear it," I said aloud.

"Quiet, Jonathan," Mrs. Vanling said. "Odd. Mrs. Delehanty is usually out here doing her paperwork at this time of day."

"Maybe she's in the kitchen," I suggested. It occurred to me that this could be the solution of a big part of our continuing problem. If the principal of our school got a look at the yogurt creature, maybe we wouldn't have to fight these rotten menaces alone anymore.

We went to the kitchen door and opened it. The gurgling noise was louder, and Mrs. Delehanty was lying unconscious on the floor, with a big, purple lump showing through her hair on the top of her head. A dented saucepan lay on the floor beside her.

Mrs. Vanling gave a little cry of distress, and ran to the assistance of the fallen teacher, but Michael, Gemma, and I ran to the big, stainless steel sink, where we saw the last of the thick gooey whiteness disappearing down the drain.

9

Mom put a pile of green beans next to my lamb chop. My mind was yelling, *Oh, no!* but by the time it left my mouth, I had managed to change it to a cheery, "Gee, we're having green beans at the banquet tomorrow, too."

"Oh, that's right," she said. "I'm sorry, Jon."

"That's okay," I said, chewing away at some. I swallowed. "Yours are better than ours are probably going to be."

Mom smiled at me. "I'll bet yours are going to be terrific." Then she frowned. "That is, if we go to this thing at all."

"But we have to," Michael blurted.

"Not with all the things that have been happening at that school, lately. I'm glad poor Mrs. Delehanty is going to be all right."

"But that was an accident. She told the police so, herself." She did. She woke up soon after Mrs. Vanling called the police. Mrs. Delehanty told them that she was absolutely alone in the room, and that there was absolutely no way anybody could have gotten behind her. Her memory was hazy, but she insisted she must have fallen and hit her head. The pan, she said, must have been dented by her knocking it off the shelf or something.

And then, while she was unconscious, somebody came in and stole the yogurt. They just left a bunch of empty pots in the refrigerator.

Well, Chief Jackson, Abdul's father, had a lot of trouble with that one, and who can blame him? Still, given what Mrs. Delehanty was telling him, that's what they had to believe.

Little did they know. One of the policemen quoted Sherlock Holmes, saying, "When you have eliminated the impossible, whatever remains, however improbable, must be the truth."

Unfortunately, in this case, you didn't dare eliminate the impossible, because that was what was happening.

An ambulance came for Mrs. Delehanty. She seemed okay, but they were taking her to the hospital for observation. At least she didn't have any signs of some terrible new disease.

I'd talked to Michael about that as soon as the three of us were alone in the back of the late bus home. He pointed out that it didn't make sense, from the Twisters' point of view, to unleash the disease until they could infect a lot of people at once. They wanted a swift, sure blow to incapacitate the town.

"Wait a minute," Gemma had said. "I thought we were working on the assumption that they could only do a teensy little time warp, only big enough to send through a little bit of bacteria. They certainly couldn't send the parts of their war machines through that. So what good would it do them to wipe out the town now?"

"I've been thinking about that," Michael said. "I think there are three possible explanations."

"Let's hear them," I said.

"One, the Twisters have enough power for one big push, and they're tired of waiting. I think that's pretty unlikely, considering what we did to their equipment."

He was bending down his fingers as he counted off the ideas. "Two, this may be the kind of disease that, you know, spreads. They may be counting on this to wipe humans out, so they don't need the war machines. Then they can come and mop up what's left of us whenever they want to."

"Nice thought. And the yogurt creature is loose in the school plumbing somewhere." I asked Michael what the third thought was.

This made him gulp. "I also thought this might be, you know, revenge. Against us, for what we did to their plans the first time."

"Oh, great," Gemma said. "As if we didn't have enough to worry about. Now we have to feel guilty about being the reason the human race gets wiped out."

"You have nothing to feel guilty about," I told her. "At least we're not going to watch all our friends and neighbors sit down and eat the stuff. You did that."

"And," Michael said, "the human race isn't going to get wiped out. I think I know how to fight this thing."

That was the reason he was so upset at the idea that Mom might decide to skip the Spring Festival. To fight the thing (and I had to admit, he had a good plan), we had to be there. And not just us—we were going to need some troops.

"I still don't like what's been going on," Mom said.

"We don't either," I said. "But if you let the Twister—" I caught myself. "I mean the twisted jerk

77

who's behind this ruin everything, then we let him win.''

That was pretty good, I thought. Gemma couldn't have done any better.

Apparently, Mom liked it, too. ''Are you going to come into the firm with me someday, Jon?'' She smiled at me. ''All right, we'll go. I hope they put a stop to this business, whoever's behind it.''

''Me, too,'' Michael said around a big hunk of lamb chop. Mom told him not to talk with his mouth full, and things were back to normal.

The next day, we got up very early, just about the time of the June sunrise. We'd spent a lot of time on the phone last night, as had Gemma, and we hoped that all over town, kids were doing the same thing.

The first thing we did was to get our Super Soaker water guns and leftover balloons from Michael's last birthday party. Then we went down to the kitchen to load them.

We decided on pine cleaner as being effective and most pleasant to deal with. We used a plastic funnel to get some in each water pistol, and in each balloon. Then we added water until we had a good, strong solution. Next, we pulled some two-liter soda bottles out of the box we keep them in to bring them back to the store, and mixed an even stronger solution in them. Mom also had a gallon of bleach in the laundry room, and we grabbed that, too.

Finally, we packed it all up in a couple of cartons, sealed them with tape, and brought them out to the car.

''Hey, Jon,'' Michael said. ''What if Mom can't drive us to school today? This stuff would be awfully heavy to carry on the bus. Besides, they don't like to have me on the bus even when I'm not lugging big cartons around.''

''Don't create problems. In my whole life, from before you were born, Mom hasn't refused to drive me to school when I asked her.''

''We've got to get the stuff there,'' Michael said.

''Right,'' I said. ''We've got to do it, so we'll do it. We'll pull it to school in your wagon, if we have to.''

Michael's face brightened up; he liked the idea.

In any case, Mom woke up happy and smiling. It was good to see her that way. For a long time after Dad died, she didn't smile much, and when she did they were sad smiles. She'd been okay for quite awhile now, but I could still remember the sad times.

I thought about what a good mom she was, working hard, but still around for us, trying to understand our problems even when she had plenty of her own.

Then I thought about the Twisters trying to kill her. Not the earth, not the town, just the woman I was lucky to have for my mother, and suddenly this fight got very personal. Michael's plan would work, because I was going to make it work. I wasn't going to let Mom down.

And of course, there was no problem about her driving us to school.

She didn't notice about the boxes until we were wrestling them out of the car.

''What in the world is *that?*'' she asked.

''Surprise for tonight,'' Michael told her.

''Oh, okay,'' she said.

We put the boxes down and waited at the main entrance for our co-conspirators. Stacy showed up first. She had a plastic bag with her brother's motorized water gun inside; she'd loaded it with straight bleach. That was fine for our purposes, but I figured it might be a little tough on her brother's toy.

Abdul and Biff were driven up in a police car by the chief himself, who personally took out a box and brought it in.

"I think it's great, what you children are doing," the chief said, and left.

"Uh, Abdul, what does he think we're doing?"

Abdul was proud of himself. "I told him we all wanted the school to be extra-special clean for the banquet, so a bunch of us were gong to help Mr. Lije by getting cleaning stuff into hard to reach places."

Then he scowled at me. "By the way," he said. "What is it we *are* doing? I took your word for it that it was important, because I trust the little genius, here. But I don't dare embarrass my dad or my mom, so I'd like to know what we're doing."

"Pretty much what you said," the little genius told him. "Except the Mr. Lije part. There's something in the school that needs to be . . . cleaned up. You'll know it when you see it."

"This whole thing is silly," Biff said. "The school is perfectly clean."

"I've seen your room," Abdul told him.

"So?"

"I know what your idea of clean is." We laughed.

Over the next few minutes, the rest of our little army of seventh graders showed up. A couple of the kids we'd called had thought we were joking, and hadn't done anything, but about seven of them had, and Michael felt that ought to be enough.

Now we were waiting for Gemma. She was worth waiting for. When she showed up, she had three suitcases.

"Gosh, Gem," said Linda Renkovic, "what are you doing, moving in?" Linda, by the way, was the best water gun shot I had ever seen.

"No," said Gemma, struggling with the bags. "I am not moving in. This is practically all water balloons. Somebody help me with this stuff, please?"

Our homeroom teacher was a little overwhelmed by the quantity of the stuff we put in the closet, but we told her it was for the banquet, and she didn't mind too much.

All the kids had come up with various excuses not to go home between the end of school and the Spring Festival, some of which were even legitimate. Between the end of school and the beginning of dinner, we'd engage the yogurt monster in a battle over the fate of our town and our planet.

We couldn't afford to lose.

19

We went into action about four P.M. It would have been easier if we'd had darkness, the way we'd had the other night, but the banquet was due to start at eight o'clock, and in June, the sun is only just going down about then in Marsdentown.

We were systematically going around the school cutting off the ways the creature could use to attack. We were pouring disinfectant down every drain in the place. The hardest part was slinking through the halls of the school carrying around huge, brightly colored water guns, pushing boxes, and dragging suitcases.

There were plenty of teachers still around, even after all the clubs had finished up; we kept dodging them, or thinking of lame excuses to give them when they saw us.

Still, we were getting the job done. Michael reasoned that the creature would most likely bring its disease-ridden carcass into the gym while everybody was eating, and, using the gas bubbles inside it, blow itself up, splattering everybody with deadly goop. Either that, or it would try to incorporate itself into the food we *were* going to eat.

That was what we took care of first. Abdul had managed to get hold of a master key to the school his father had for security reasons ("I could get grounded the rest of my life if my dad finds out I took this," he said), so access was no problem.

First we went to the home ec kitchen, where Michael took a sample of the tofu and went over to the chem lab to check it out under the microscope to make sure that was okay. Meanwhile, I disinfected the yogurt vat and all the sinks, especially the one the monster had fled through before.

Michael came back with the news that the tofu burgers would be okay.

Next, we hit the cafeteria kitchen, where the food would be prepared. Then we worked our way through the school.

"Why don't we just pour it down all of the sinks?" Stacy asked.

Stacy had surprised me. She never struck me as the housework type, but she was working as hard as anybody. Maybe harder. I didn't care if she always arranged things so that she was closer to Biff than Linda was; the work was getting done.

Michael could have explained why we were leaving the drain in the boys' room undone. He'd already explained it to me last night, when I'd asked him the same question Stacy had. The reason was that we couldn't be sure how deep into the pipes the germ-killing stuff would work. We wanted to force it out, where we could get at it.

"But, Michael," I had said, "what if it just goes down the pipes and comes up in somebody's house?"

Michael had thought of that already. "I don't think it can leave the school," he said. "It's had plenty of chances just to get us on the schoolyard, and a lot of parents, too, like the other night when we chased it around. But it never has."

"I hope that holds true," I said.

"Me, too."

Over the next half hour, squirt guns at the ready, lugging our supply of germ-killing water balloons, we proceeded to disinfect the rest of the school.

All but one drain—the one in the floor of the boys' bathroom near the east door, the one down which we'd seen it disappear. That one, we surrounded.

I at first suggested that the girls stand guard outside, but that didn't go over so well.

"You're not going to keep us out of the action," Linda said.

"You don't even know what the action *is* yet," Gemma pointed out.

"Well," Stacy said, "it must be something exciting, if we've got all this firepower, mustn't it, Biff?"

Gemma said, "Water power, actually."

Biff said, "Huh?"

"Okay, okay," I said. "I just thought you'd feel a little funny about hanging around a boys' room."

I said that, because as dumb as it sounds, I still felt funny about being in the girls' room the other night. Obviously, none of my allies felt that way, or at least none of them would admit it.

Finally, Bob Blair said he'd be the lookout. Bob is the shortest boy in seventh grade, but he's also the fastest. He's a backup infielder on the baseball team, and the number one pinch runner.

"Leave your water gun inside the door," Michael said.

"Right." Bob slipped outside.

We sat around and waited, watching the drain. Time went by, a lot of it. Cars started pulling up in the parking lot outside, probably the cafeteria workers on their way to prepare the meal. We talked quietly while we waited.

"One thing," Abdul said. "The school is starting to smell better already."

"Another good thing," Linda said. "Ice cream for dessert instead of yogurt."

She went on to explain how Mrs. Vanling had gotten in touch with the mother of a third grader. The family had an ice cream store, and they agreed to provide the dessert in the absence of the yogurt at a really great price. Not only that, but because it hadn't been budgeted for, Mr. Calstone had agreed to pay for it out of his own pocket, and take his chances on the school board paying him back.

"Well," Abdul said. "Three cheers for Mr. Calstone! And I never thought I'd say that."

If you've never spent a couple of hours looking at a drain, let me tell you, it's boring. Even if you're expecting a monster to come up out of it. The rest of the kids, who'd just been told we had to wait there for something, were starting to get a little peeved.

"Is this a joke, Jon?" Biff demanded.

"I wish," I said.

"No joke," Gemma echoed.

There was a little grumbling. I was glad we were all headed to the banquet after this. They might grumble, but they weren't going to walk out on us, because they had to hang around the school anyway.

Bob was back in the hallway on guard duty—we'd been switching off. Just as I started a yawn big enough to crack my jaw, we heard his voice from outside.

"*Holy macaroni!*"

There was a special tone in his voice that let us know he'd really seen something.

Michael was the first one to join him. In my eagerness to join them I practically pushed Biff and Stacy (she was still sort of drifting to his side) out of the door ahead of me. I, in turn, was jostled by the rest.

Bob pointed down the hallway, but he didn't need to. It's hard to miss an eight foot tall blob of whiteness in the rough shape of a man.

"What the heck is *that?*" Abdul demanded.

"That's why you're having ice cream tonight," Gemma said.

I had my own question. "Michael, what is it doing down *there?*"

Michael looked sick. "I guess we missed one. Does Mrs. Vanling have her own bathroom?"

"Of course she does," Abdul said. "My mother uses it all the time."

Michael made a noise that sounded like *guuuuuh.*

"All right," I said. "Gemma, pour some disinfectant down the drain we've been guarding. Everybody grab your stuff. The trap didn't work; we'll have to go chase it."

Gemma said, "Um, I don't think we're going to have to do that, Jon. I think it's chasing us."

She was right. When we had seen it, it had "seen" us. It was coming at us now, and fast, sliding its fake "feet" along the floor as if it were skating.

Gemma disappeared, fixed the drain, and came back,

and we were still all standing there, watching it come down the long hallway.

"It's got to get us," Michael said. "Now that we've seen it. That it knows we're out to get it first."

"What—what are we giong to do?" someone asked.

"Well, we're not going to stand here and wait for it to get us!" Gemma said. She unzipped her suitcase, grabbed a couple of water balloons, and ran up the hallway to meet it.

That's all it took. Just one person with guts. With a bunch of wordless battle cries, we grabbed our weaponry and followed.

We got to Gemma just as she heaved her water balloons. They squished a little into the creature, but bounced off him without breaking.

They did break when they hit the floor, though, and the chlorine bleach scented water made the creature slide back in alarm.

That gave me an idea. I tossed a couple of water balloons of my own, lofting them high.

"You missed him," Stacy said as they splatted open on the floor behind the creature.

"I meant to," I said. "He hates disinfectant. Soak the floor all around him, cut off attack *and* retreat."

We did. Ten more water balloons, and the creature was surrounded by a pool of bacteria-killing water. It's feet were liquifying; it was a little shorter than it had been.

Then Biff got an idea. He took a running start, then threw a water balloon so it smashed on the floor a couple of feet in front of the creature, splashing disinfectant liquid up as far as where its belly would be if it had one. That brought on the bubbling scream Gemma, Michael, and I had heard night before last.

"That hurt it," Michael said. "Keep it up."

Nobody was stopping. All the while this had been going on, we had been hitting it with our Super Soakers, watching the thin streams of treated water cutting deep into the whiteness. Linda was living up to her reputation as a great shot by keeping the stream concentrated on the creature's face. Not that any place was any more vulnerable than any other, but the tight grin on her lips made it look as though she was enjoying it.

We were beating it. It was shrinking before our eyes, like the Wicked Witch in the Wizard of Oz. "All right," I heard Gemma say, as she smashed a water balloon against the ceiling and let the disinfectant drizzle down on top of the monster. "All right," she said again.

Then the creature did something none of us could have anticipated.

It grew a long white arm, then brought it forward in an overhand motion, as if it were trying to throw something at us.

It was. It was throwing the arm.

It came loose from the main body of the creature, and in the air, broke up into three blobs.

"Look out!" Michael yelled. "Don't let it touch you!"

That was easier said than done. Everybody managed to duck the yogurt-puppies while they were in the air, but as soon as they hit, they formed up into miniatures of the big one, and came to attack us.

"Look out, Jon!" Abdul yelled, and blasted one away from my leg with his soaker.

I yelled a quick thanks, and passed the favor along to Bob, who was so busy fighting the big one, he wasn't even aware the little ones had started.

The third one left off attacking, and tried to escape,

but Gemma cut it off with a water balloon, and Linda dissolved it with a great piece of long-range shooting.

We turned our attention back to the big one.

"Keep shooting for the edges," I said. "Don't let it do that again."

But it didn't try to do that again. We'd soaked it with too much of the stuff that was killing it. It dissolved slowly, whitening the solutions we'd used to get it. The bubble-scream grew lower and quieter, then stopped altogether, but we kept soaking it until it was completely liquified, and even after.

Finally, it was all gone.

For a long minute, nobody said anything. We just stood there, breathing heavily, and looking at each other. Gemma managed a weak grin; I was able to return it.

It was Abdul who broke the silence. "What the heck *was* that thing?" he demanded.

"Remember what we told you last winter?" Michael said. "When we went through the Twisters' time warp? Well, this was their attempt at revenge."

"Oh, come *off* it," Stacy said. "This was no time warp. It was something we could see right here. What was it really, Gem?"

This was the point where Gemma usually crushed Stacy with a sarcastic remark, but this time I guess she was too drained.

"Never mind that," she said. "We've got to get this mess cleaned up, and change into some dry clothes so we can go to the dinner."

And about forty-five minutes and half a million paper towels later, that's exactly what we did.

Mom and the Davises were already at our table when we went to meet them. Mom looked so pretty and so happy to see us, that Michael and I gave her a big hug. We were happy to see her, and even happier to know we could go on seeing her.

"Well," she said, "this is a nice surprise." Then she sniffed and said, "You smell like bleach."

"We've been doing some cleaning up," Gemma said.

Gemma's dad ruffled her hair and said, "How do we get you to do that at home?"

"You don't want to know, Dad," she said.

Actually, if Mom had sniffed us a little more closely, she would have detected pine cleaner, household disinfectant, and all the rest on us, too.

The bleach was strongest because, at Michael's insistence, after we soaked up the stuff with the paper towels, we soaked all the paper towels in bleach, just to make sure every single bacterium was dead. We wore rubber gloves while we did this. We got them from the

90

same place we got the bleach—Mr. Lije's supply room, courtesy of Abdul's master key.

We were glad we had told everyone to bring a change of clothes, because we were wet. This time, we went to separate bathrooms to change before going down to the gym to join the folks.

On the way down, there was all kinds of speculation.

"I know," Biff said. "It was something the little genius whipped up in the lab. World's youngest mad scientist."

"That's not funny," Michael said, but the rest of us got a laugh out of it. Especially Stacy.

"Is she being obvious, or what?" I whispered to Gemma.

"It's not so easy to get a boy to notice if you like him," she said.

"Well, why doesn't she just *tell* him?"

"It's—it must be scary, just to put it out there like that. Don't you think?"

I shrugged. "I suppose so," I said.

Gemma just said, "Yeah."

By the time the tofu burgers came, we were ready for them. The thing was, not to think of them as supposing to taste like hamburgers. If you remembered that, then they were completely edible. Ketchup drowned out the taste of them, anyway.

There were speeches and awards and stuff. Gemma won one as the school's outstanding musician, and we were all proud of her.

I don't know when the thought first came to me. One second I was sitting there, feeling pretty darned good, and then something began to tickle in my brain. The tickle became an itch, and it was well on its way to becoming an actual pain.

I leaned over and whispered to my brother, "Michael, you have to go to the bathroom."

"No, I don't," he said.

"Yes, you do. I want to talk to you, in private."

Michael looked doubtful, but he played along. He announced he had to go, but he didn't want to go alone through the empty school. I volunteered to take him. Since Gemma knew that Michael had caused us to sneak into the school late at night to go fight a monster, she knew Michael wasn't seriously afraid, and she gave me a curious look as we left the table. For the first time in my life, I wished she was a boy, so she could be in on this conference, too.

Michael and I didn't actually go to the bathroom. As far as I was concerned, we'd spent way too much time hanging around in the boys' room over the last few days as it was. We just went a little way down the corridor and talked in low voices.

"What is it, Jon?" my brother asked.

"I thought of something."

"What's that? We got all of the monster, honest."

"Maybe not," I said.

"That bleach did it, I'm sure of it."

"That's not what I'm talking about." I was getting excited. I took a deep breath and went on. "Here's what I'm wondering: Why was the monster shaped the way it was?"

"What do you mean?"

"Why was it shaped like a *person?* It was a pile of milk and bacteria, wasn't it? Why should it form itself into a human shape? It would have been better off as a blob."

"It turned into a Twister once."

"I know. When we hurt it the first time, with the bleach bottles."

"Like you said, Jon, bacteria can't think. The Twisters had to have been controlling it. Some kind of mental projection, is what I figure."

"And I'm sure you're right," I told him. "But if the Twisters were in direct control, wouldn't it make sense for the creature to be shaped like a Twister *all the time?*"

The genius finally made the connection. "Of course," he breathed. "And it must take a lot of energy to project even mental force across a time warp. They must have taken control of somebody when the clocks went crazy, the same time they warped the bacteria through."

"Any candidates?" I asked.

He gave me a grin. "That's not hard, Jon. I *thought* he was too nice to be true."

"What are we going to do?"

"We'll have to watch him."

"Forever?" I think my voice squeaked. I had other plans for my future than to keep an eye on a possible Twister agent.

"At least tonight," Michael said. "Half of the town is still here in one place."

I swallowed hard. I hadn't even thought of that.

"We'd better tell the rest of the kids."

Michael shook his head. "You saw how they were acting after we got rid of the monster. By Monday, they'll be believing it was a special effects rehearsal for a movie, or that we were testing a new action game or something."

"Well, we've got to tell Gemma."

Michael looked at me as if I were crazy. "*She's* not one of the rest of the kids," he said. "She's one of *us*."

93

It wasn't easy keeping one eye on the head table where Mr. Calstone was, and trying to make an opportunity to tell Gemma what was going on. Finally, smart kid that she was, she provided it. I was watching her as she accidentally-on-purpose spilled her lemonade on the floor.

I sprang to help her clean it up, totally astonishing my mother, who had her mouth open to tell me to do it, but didn't get the chance.

After a whispered explanation, Gemma made a face and said, "I knew it was too easy."

"*Easy?*" I almost yelled it.

"*Sssssssh!*"

I lowered my voice to a harsh whisper. "That was easy to you? I was scared to death."

"So was I. I just had trouble believing it was over. All right, we watch Mr. Calstone. Then what?"

"I don't know. One thing at a time."

"Yeah." In a normal voice, Gemma said, "Thanks for helping me, Jon."

"Glad to," I said. We sounded so phony, I was surprised when we didn't get suspicious looks from our parents.

After the soy-burgers and the green beans (which were delicious, by the way) and the rest of the main meal was gone, but before dessert, it was time for the ecology pageants put on by a couple of the grades.

I'd tell you about them, but I can't because I didn't see them. That was just about the time Mr. Calstone got up from the head table and left the room.

I was going to bolt up and follow him, but Michael kicked me under the table, and I realized it made sense to give the assistant principal a little bit of a head start.

A few seconds after Mr. Calstone was out the door,

Michael said he had to go again. I thought he was wearing that excuse out a little, but Mom only wondered if he were coming down with something.

She felt his forehead, and was happy with his temperature. "Don't be so sour, Jon," Mom said. "You get taken care of, too."

I wasn't sour; I was anxious that Mr. Calstone was getting too big a head start. I practically picked Michael up and carried him out of there.

Gemma joined us before we'd even made it to the main building. I never did find out what she told her parents.

"Where is he?" she asked.

I said I didn't know; Michael said he'd be at the main entrance.

"How do you know that?"

"It's time for the ice cream to be delivered."

"There's no cover there," I said. "How are we going to watch him?"

We thought that one over for a few seconds. Then Gemma said, "We'll follow him at a distance. If he sees us, I'll think of something to tell him."

We made it to the corner of the T, looked around, and there was Mr. Calstone, leaning against a wall, whistling. He didn't look like someone in the control of hostile aliens, but yogurt doesn't ordinarily look like a weapon of world conquest, either.

Michael said, "Wait here," and slipped away into the semi-darkness of the corridor. So much for the kid who was afraid to go to the bathroom by himself.

He came back before Mr. Calstone had any company.

"Here," he said, and pushed something into my hand.

I looked at it. It was his mini-soaker, about the size of a regular water pistol, but still battery powered.

"I had this in my locker, just in case."

Just in case of what? I wondered. Just in case we got chased down this way by the monster? Just in case we needed to blast the assistant principal with a water pistol? Geniuses are hard to figure out.

The road behind the main entrance windows lit up, and a brightly colored station wagon drove up. We could see now that in the recess behind him, Mr. Calstone had a wheeled pushcart. A man got out of the truck, and he and Mr. Calstone loaded big three-gallon drums of ice cream onto it. Then we saw Mr. Calstone hand the man a check. The man got back in the car and drove off.

That's when we realized we had no place to hide; that if he wheeled the ice cream back to the gym, he was bound to see us. Our only choice was if we wanted him to see us running away, or as the smiling nice children we were.

It was Gemma's call, and she made it. She popped out and said, "Hi, Mr. Calstone. We figured this was what you left the dinner about. Need any help?"

He smiled at us. I wondered why the Twisters made him smile so much. "Not really, kids, but I'm glad to have the company. What flavor do you like?"

We didn't get a chance to answer him, because Mrs. Vanling was coming up the hallway. We thought she'd be mad, but she wasn't.

"Oh, Homer, good, I'm glad it's here. Did you enter it in the ledger?"

"No, I didn't, Marjorie. Since I was paying for it myself, I didn't think I needed to."

Mrs. Vanling shrugged. "Technically, it's a delivery of food to the school, and it has to be recorded. State law, you know. Look, I'll do it."

"Oh, no," Mr. Calstone began.

"Yes, you've missed enough of the party already. You go on back. I'm sure the children will help me out—they'll want to keep their eyes on the ice cream."

Most of the time, she'd have been right, but not now.

Gemma tried to weasel us out of it, but Mrs. Vanling wouldn't hear of it. So, with a sick feeling in our stomachs, we followed the ice cream back to the principal's office to be logged in, while our main suspect disappeared down the hallway where the rest of the town waited.

Mrs. Vanling brought us into the office and said, "Sit down for a minute children, then we can get started." She went back out and wheeled in the ice cream, then ignored it for a moment, and sat behind her desk.

"Mrs. Vanling," Gemma said, "would it be possible for one of us to stay and help you while the other brings Michael back to his mother? She might be getting worried."

Mrs. Vanling smiled her pretty smile. "Mr. Calstone will take care of that."

That's what we were afraid of.

"I miss my mom," Michael tried.

"Don't be silly, children. The sooner we're done with what we have to do, the sooner you can rejoin your parents."

"All right, ma'am," I said. "What do you want me to do? Read off the flavors while you write them down?"

"I'll take care of the ice cream. I just want to reassure you."

"About what?" Gemma asked.

"About Mr. Calstone. You think his mind is being controlled by an alien race you call the Twisters. You don't have to worry. It isn't."

"Oh, no," I said.

"Oh, yes, Jon," she said. "When the message came, his mind was not prepared for it. All it did was alter his personality, remove some of the anger and frustration he had built up over the years.

"But I was here, too, you know, and I was able to accept that wonderful gift."

"Gift?" Michael said. "They're just using you!"

"Using me? Nonsense. They're going to recreate the earth."

"Yeah," said Gemma. "Recreate it with no people on it."

I was closest to the door. I though of making a break for it, but it was as if Mrs. Vanling read my mind.

"I wouldn't try it, Jon. I have the means to stop you, and I will."

"Mrs. Vanling," I tried, "you're a human being. This isn't really you."

She smiled happily. "Now it is," she said. The smile went away, and she continued. "You know, you three have really vexed me. First you prevented me from serving up the creature to the town. Those veiled threats of lawsuits were very clever, Gemma. I had to go along with them, or Mr. Calstone would be suspicious, however kindly he's become."

Now I knew why the Twisters needed to work through a human. Not just to shape and to control the creature, but to know about earth things like lawsuits.

"Secondly, you made me have the creature hurt Mrs. Delehanty. That worked out all right; she didn't even believe what she knew had happened to her. And third, you destroyed my creature utterly, thereby preventing me from sending it to the banquet.

"From your use of the disinfectants, I know you've guessed that the plan is to spread a disease. I don't know what the symptoms will be, but I do know it will be deadly.''

"You mean your plan *was* to spread disease," Michael said. "Whatever you do to us, you can't bring your monster back."

She shook her head and spoke softly. She might have been telling us that the field was too wet for outside recess today. "No," she said. "I can't bring it back. But I do have this."

She reached into a desk drawer and pulled out a quart jar full of some jellylike stuff that glowed pale blue, the way some bacteria cultures do. I never heard of one as bright as this, though.

"Do you really think I would send my creature out to face you without drawing off some of the concentrated essence of the mutated bacteria? *This*," she said, holding the jar aloft, "will be injected into the ice cream, and the original plan will come to fruition after all."

She stood up from her desk. "But I'm curious. I'd like to know what the symptoms are. I think I'll try it out on you three right here." She began to unscrew the lid. "I'm sure it will be fast-acting. If not, I'll just have to wait until the whole town gets the disease."

"Won't you get it, too?"

She thought about it for a moment. "Perhaps," she said with a shrug. "It doesn't matter. My job will be done, and my masters will own the earth!"

The jar was open, now. She got up from behind the desk and walked toward us.

12

Gemma gave me a look that said, "Get ready." Then she screamed.

It gave me the opening I needed. When Mrs. Vanling looked at Gemma, I pulled the water pistol out of my pocket.

I don't ordinarily, recommend blasting your principal in the face with a super soaker, especially one loaded with a pine cleaner solution, but in this case it worked.

Because it didn't matter if the Twisters had her under control, she was still in a human body, and getting that stuff in the eyes and mouth is going to cause any human body to react. Mrs. Vanling dropped the jar and grabbed her face.

Then she collapsed to the floor. I thought I'd killed her; but she started moaning, so I knew I hadn't. Cautiously, I approached her.

Just then, Michael and Gemma both screamed. I turned around and screamed, too. The jar hadn't broken when it hit the carpeted floor of the office, but the top had been loose. Glowing blue gunk was oozing slowly out of it, and it seemed to be crawling toward my brother and Gemma.

I raised the soaker and was about to blast it, when Michael said, "No!"

"What do you mean, *no?*" I yelled. "Are you nuts?"

"You might splash it; we might not find all the pieces."

He was right, as usual. While Gemma went to see about Mrs. Vanling, I used the soaker to drench the carpet around the disease culture. Then, reducing the force of the spray, I hit it with more and more disinfectant solution until the glow was gone, and the little, deadly blob had completely liquified.

As the last glimmer of blue disappeared, Mrs. Vanling moaned, "No . . . no . . ." Then she began to shake, as if she were freezing in the middle of June.

"She's getting her own brain back," Michael said. "The Twisters' influence was all tied up with the bacteria. Once the last of that was gone, so was their control."

"How can you know that?" Gemma demanded.

"I don't know it. It's a hypothesis."

Right after he said that, Mrs. Vanling justified it. All the nastiness was gone from her. She seemed very tired and weak, but with an almost unbelievable effort, she raised her head from the floor and looked around. Gemma helped to hold her head up.

"Gemma," Mrs. Vanling said in a weak voice. "Michael. Jonathan. Thank you. You . . . you have given me back to myself. I'm sorry for the trouble I caused. I—"

Her head went limp.

Michael whispered, "Oh, no," and started to cry. So did Gemma, and I got pretty misty myself.

13

Now before you go getting as nervous as we were, I'd better tell you that she wasn't dead. In fact, not only wasn't she dead, she didn't even stay in the hospital that long.

Even while we were still blubbering, Gemma detected a pulse in Mrs. Vanling's neck. I went to call 911, and Michael ran back to the gym to get help. The ambulance guys tried to shoo us out, but we didn't move until one of them said Mrs. Vanling was in no danger, and they took her away.

We went back to the gym, where Mr. Calstone announced that Mrs. Vanling had collapsed, but she was going to be okay. I heard one of the kids say that the yogurt fumes finally got her, but his humor was not appreciated. We went ahead and ate the ice cream and finished the ecology program, because that was what Mrs. Vanling would have wanted us to do.

A few days later, we were hanging around Gemma's house playing Grape Escape. It's a babyish game, but Michael loves squishing the grapes.

"My mom says that Mrs. Vanling got out of the

hospital today." Mrs. Davis went to the hospital a couple of times a week to do the maintenance on their computers and printers and copiers and stuff, so she knew everything that was going on there.

"That's good," I said. "I was worried about her."

"Yeah," Michael said. "Me, too. Since Mr. Calstone's been acting principal, the school is like getting sent to prison every day."

I grinned. "He is awfully strict. But he's nicer about it than he used to be."

Gemma said, "If he stayed completely nice, I'd worry that the Twisters were still doing things, somehow."

"Good point," Michael said. "I think we're safe from them, now, for a while."

"Yeah," I sighed. "For a while. When does Mrs. Vanling get back?"

"She should be back before the end of the school year," Gemma said. "The official explanation of what happened to her is 'stress.' "

"Well, I bet it *is* pretty stressful to have alien monsters take over your brain and try to get you to kill your whole town with a disgusting disease," Michael said.

Gemma and I admitted that we had found it pretty stressful, and we weren't even the ones whose brains had been taken over.

"According to my mother," Gemma said, "Mrs. Vanling's husband says she was acting a little strangely the past few days, and that he should have noticed something."

I laughed. "We might have noticed something if we hadn't been so hypnotized by the change in Mr. Calstone. Anyway, I want to talk to Mrs. Vanling as soon as she gets back to work. With a grownup who knows about the Twisters on our side, we can be more effective the next time.''

Michael was angry. He gave the Play-Do grape another stomp from the boot machine and said, ''We were effective. We saved the earth. For the second time!''

''It would be nice,'' Gemma said gently, ''to have more help. Unfortunately, it's not going to happen.''

''Why not?'' I demanded. ''She must hate the Twisters worse than we do.''

''Because according to my mother, the doctors say Mrs. Vanling has no memory of the last week and a half.''

I would have been more disappointed, but down deep I must have been expecting it.

''Okay, then, it's still just us against the Twisters.''

''Don't forget Biff and Stacy and Abdul and Linda and Bob and the rest of them,'' Michael said. ''They may not believe their eyes, but they did help when the chips were down.''

''That's true,'' Gemma said. ''And we've always got each other. We're a darn good team.''

''Sure are,'' I said. ''As Michael said, we saved the earth twice. No reason we can't go on doing it as often as we need to.'' Not that I was hoping we'd need to.

''But we can't do it on an empty stomach,'' Michael hinted. ''Is there anything to eat around here?''

''Michael,'' I told him, ''if Mom heard you say that, she'd send you to your room.''

''It's okay,'' Gemma said. ''I'm pretty hungry myself. My mom's got some yogurt in the refrigerator,'' she said. ''Feel brave enough to eat it?''

''Sure,'' I said with a grin. ''Nothing scares us.''

So, laughing, we went downstairs to get some yogurt, the Snack of Heroes.

IF YOU DARE TO BE SCARED... READ SPINETINGLERS!

by M.T. COFFIN

(#1) THE SUBSTITUTE CREATURE
77829-7/$3.50 US/$4.50 Can

(#2) BILLY BAKER'S DOG WON'T STAY BURIED
77742-8/$3.50 US/$4.50 Can

(#3) MY TEACHER'S A BUG
77785-1/$3.50 US/$4.50 Can

(#4) WHERE HAVE ALL THE PARENTS GONE?
78117-4/$3.50 US/$4.50 Can

(#5) CHECK IT OUT—AND DIE!
78116-6/$3.50 US/$4.50 Can

(#6) SIMON SAYS, "CROAK!"
78232-4/$3.50 US/$4.50 Can

(#7) SNOW DAY
78157-3/$3.50 US/$4.50 Can

(#8) DON'T GO TO THE PRINCIPAL'S OFFICE
78313-4/$3.50 US/$4.99 Can

(#9) STEP ON A CRACK
78432-7/$3.50 US/$4.99 Can

Buy these books at your local bookstore or use this coupon for ordering:

Mail to: Avon Books, Dept BP, Box 767, Rte 2, Dresden, TN 38225   E
Please send me the book(s) I have checked above.
❏ My check or money order—no cash or CODs please—for $_____ is enclosed (please
add $1.50 per order to cover postage and handling—Canadian residents add 7% GST).
❏ Charge my VISA/MC Acct#_____Exp Date_____
Minimum credit card order is two books or $7.50 (please add postage and handling
charge of $1.50 per order—Canadian residents add 7% GST). For faster service, call
1-800-762-0779. Residents of Tennessee, please call 1-800-633-1607. Prices and numbers are
subject to change without notice. Please allow six to eight weeks for delivery.

Name_____
Address_____
City_____State/Zip_____
Telephone No._____   MTC 0196

Join in the Wild and Crazy Adventures with Some Trouble-Making Plants

by Nancy McArthur

THE PLANT THAT ATE DIRTY SOCKS
75493-2/ $3.99 US/ $5.50 Can

THE RETURN OF THE PLANT THAT ATE DIRTY SOCKS
75873-3/ $3.99 US/ $5.50 Can

THE ESCAPE OF THE PLANT THAT ATE DIRTY SOCKS
76756-2/ $3.50 US/ $4.25 Can

THE SECRET OF THE PLANT THAT ATE DIRTY SOCKS
76757-0/ $3.50 US/ $4.50 Can

MORE ADVENTURES OF THE PLANT THAT ATE DIRTY SOCKS
77663-4/ $3.50 US/ $4.50 Can

THE PLANT THAT ATE DIRTY SOCKS GOES UP IN SPACE
77664-2/ $3.99 US/ $5.50 Can

Buy these books at your local bookstore or use this coupon for ordering:

Mail to: Avon Books, Dept BP, Box 767, Rte 2, Dresden, TN 38225   E
Please send me the book(s) I have checked above.
❑ My check or money order—no cash or CODs please—for $_____is enclosed (please add $1.50 per order to cover postage and handling—Canadian residents add 7% GST).
❑ Charge my VISA/MC Acct#_____Exp Date_____
Minimum credit card order is two books or $7.50 (please add postage and handling charge of $1.50 per order—Canadian residents add 7% GST). For faster service, call 1-800-762-0779. Residents of Tennessee, please call 1-800-633-1607. Prices and numbers are subject to change without notice. Please allow six to eight weeks for delivery.

Name_____
Address_____
City_____State/Zip_____
Telephone No._____   ESC 1095